RELIGION AND TERRORISM

RELIGION AND TERRORISM

An Interfaith Perspective

Aref M. Al-Khattar

Foreword by Vincent Moore

PRAEGER

Westport, Connecticut
London

Library of Congress Cataloging-in-Publication Data

Al-Khattar, Aref M., 1954–
  Religion and terrorism : an interfaith perspective / Aref M. Al-Khattar ; foreword by
Vincent Moore.
      p. cm.
  Includes bibliographical references and index.
  ISBN 0–275–96923–1 (alk. paper)
    1. Terrorism—Religious aspects. 2. Violence—Religious aspects. 3. Crime—
Religious aspects. 4. Religion and politics. 5. Terrorism—Prevention. I. Title.

HV6431 .A435 2003
303.6'25—dc21   2002026959

British Library Cataloguing in Publication Data is available.

Library of Congress Catalog Card Number: 2002026959
ISBN: 0–275–96923–1

First published in 2003

Praeger Publishers, 88 Post Road West, Westport, CT 06881
An imprint of Greenwood Publishing Group, Inc.
www.praeger.com

Printed in the United States of America

The paper used in this book complies with the
Permanent Paper Standard issued by the National
Information Standards Organization (Z39.48-1984).

10 9 8 7 6 5 4 3 2 1

To my family

Contents

Part III Theoretical Understanding

Foreword

Since the September 11, 2001 attacks, Americans have suddenly become aware of terrorism, although it has happened before in this country and has long been part of world history. Despite such terrorist attacks as the Oklahoma City bombing, the Unabomber's campaign of mail bombs, the arson and bombings of abortion clinics, and the 1993 bombing of the World Trade Center, America is finally waking up to this method of war because of September 11.

Terrorism is based on terror. Terror is the dread of what could happen. For the terrorist, fear is the great equalizer—not democracy, religion, education, or anything else. Whatever the goal of the perpetrator may be, terrorist acts rarely, if ever, achieve that goal. Instead they create an environment of fear. This anxiety affects large populations and the terrorist's effort, then, is disproportionately small compared to the end result.

For a more common and much less threatening analogy, consider the fear caused by a computer virus warning. If you have e-mail, you have probably received countless forwards from well-meaning friends who heard about a killer computer virus. In most cases, there is no such virus. It is much easier for a hoaxer to write an e-mail claiming there is a super virus than it is to actually write and distribute the virus. The end result, however, is fear and the individual responsible for the hoax achieves his or her end of causing a panic, without trying very hard.

Terrorists have a greater goal than merely upsetting the technophobic population about their PCs. They want to tear down and destroy a way of life in order to impose their own ideologies, which can be very specific or incredibly vague, reflecting an unclear dissatisfaction with the way things are. Religious terrorism can fall into either category, as is described in this book. While more extreme than a computer virus hoax, the goal in both cases is to cause fear.

Dr. Aref Al-Khattar examines religious-based terrorism as a way to understand the problem and possibly provide avenues to deal with it. As research for this book, he questioned leaders from three major religions, Judaism, Christianity, and Islam, about terrorism (details are in the Appendix). With this data and from his own extensive knowledge of terrorism gained from seventeen years in law enforcement, he presents a theory from an authoritative perspective.

Dr. Al-Khattar spent, as noted, seventeen years in counterterrorism with the Jordanian Department of Intelligence. After that, he earned a Master's and a Ph.D. in Criminology at Indiana University of Pennsylvania. His dissertation became this book and, while significant when submitted for his doctorate in 1998, it is even more timely now. He teaches Criminology and Criminal Justice at California University of Pennsylvania. He is a devoted husband and father of four.

Vincent Moore, Ph.D.
Assistant Professor of English
Department of Arts and Sciences
Tiffin University
Tiffin, OH

Preface

The original idea of this book started a few years ago as a dissertation project when I was in graduate school. Dr. Tim Austin, my dissertation advisor, and I spent hours and hours of discussion on the problem of terrorism. From my readings on the topic I discovered that religious-based terrorism was one of the least researched aspects of this area, so I decided to do my examination on this topic.

The unspeakable terrorist attacks of September 11, 2001 on American soil have brought the issue of religious-based terrorism under thorough investigation by the public and the law enforcement community. These acts served as a "wake-up call" to remind the public of the importance of dealing with terrorism not only in one country, but worldwide. Many people all over the world wanted to know how that happened. Questions on this issue remain unanswered—like what is the relationship between religions and terrorism, how can this violence be defined, how do terrorists justify their violence, and how can we deal with this menace? This book is an endeavor to provide some answers to these questions.

This book is divided into several major parts: Part I, "Overview," is written to inform the reader about religion, terrorism, and the relationship between these topics. The last section of this part talks about doing research on terrorism. Most information in this part comes from reviewing the literature.

Part II, "Religious Leaders Speak," includes the primary data of the book. It displays data collected from religious leaders from three religions (Judaism, Christianity, and Islam) in the United States. Participants in this project gave detailed answers to questions such as, "How do you define terrorism?" "How terrorists can justify their acts in the name of religion?" and "What can we do to counter terrorism?" Thus, in this part the reader will know about how those leaders define terrorism, each religion's justification of violence, and policy implications of these findings.

Part III, "Theoretical Understanding," takes the research questions and the participants' answers from a criminological perspective to understand the whole topic. It introduces the reader to one of the criminological theories that may explain terrorism. The author applies "Techniques of Neutralization Theory" as the theory of choice to explain religious-based terrorism based on what the primary data reveals. Readers will find how terrorists may use the process of justification provided by this theory to rationalize their violent acts.

In short, this part deals with terrorists as traditional criminals regardless of their goals. The conclusion and recommendation section of this part sums up the issue of religious based terrorism in the three religions. It provides comparison between the participants' answers and suggestions for future research on this topic.

The appendix shows the reader how the author collected the primary data for this book. It explains the qualitative nature of this research and why the author chose this method. Moreover, it details all the procedures that took place in interviewing the participants in this study.

Having said the above, it is time to recognize a few important people who helped in completing this book. I wish to express my gratitude to Dr. Tim Austin for being a great advisor; without his generous help this book would never have been published. I am especially grateful to him for his continuous emotional and intellectual support and his faith in my ability to complete this project. I am indebted to Dr. Vincent Moore, who kindly agreed to edit the final draft of this book; without his help this book would never have been completed on time. The primary data was obtained from interviews and I am very grateful to those who participated in the study and gave generously of their time and expertise to enhance the validity of this book.

I am also indebted to a number of friends and colleagues who read, criticized, and supported me: Drs. Nashat Zuraikat, Cathy Dugan, John C. Thomas, Robert J. Mutchnick, Daniel N. Boone, Thaer al-Kadi, Laila el-Omari, and Judy Sturgess.

At Greenwood Publishing Group, Dr. Heather R. Staines must be recognized for her help to publish this book in its final form.

Part I

Overview

Chapter 1

Introduction

"It is not the bullet with my name on it that worries me. It is the one that says to whom it may concern."

—Unnamed resident of Northern Ireland

The catastrophic events of September 11, 2001, in the United States—which have been called the worst terrorist acts in history—have shown the need for changes in the way we deal with terrorism in the criminal justice system and in society. Recently, changes in laws, procedures, and enforcement have taken place in almost every part of the government. However, more attention still is needed to understand how terrorists justify their violent acts not only against their victims but also for themselves. In other words, how can a person go to his/her death smiling without any kind of hesitation?

The entire world now knows that the primary suspect behind the September 11 terrorist acts is Osama Bin Laden and his organization Al Qaeda. Americans now recognize these names immediately. Nevertheless, these names were well known before September 2001 to many criminal justice systems around the world due to their alleged involvement in a number of terrorist acts around the globe.

On May 29, 2001, a federal district court in Manhattan convicted four men of conspiring with Osama Bin Laden to bomb the American embassies in Kenya and Tanzania in 1998. The bombing of these embassies in Africa made it to the *Guinness Book of World Records 2000* (Millennium Edition, p. 190) because of its severe results: 243 people were killed, the highest death toll from terrorist action against an embassy, and because of the biggest reward, $5 million, for counterterrorism that the U.S. State Department offered after the bombing. The State Department appealed for information on Osama Bin Laden, who was believed to have been behind the bombing. *The New York Times* (May 30, 2001) states that the above federal case, placed the four defendants in a global conspiracy led by Mr. Bin Laden and was rooted in Islamic fundamentalism and a hatred of Americans. Bin Laden is accused of "financing

Islamic terrorism around the world" through his own organization "Al Qaeda," an Arabic word for "base" (*New York Times,* May 30, 2001). Bin Laden is said to have inherited around $300 million that he uses to finance his activities through "moneymaking front organizations" (U.S. Department of State, April 2001).

Bin Laden's organization, according to the U.S. State Department, is a designated foreign terrorist organization. Bin Laden established this organization in the 1980s to bring together Arabs who fought in Afghanistan against the Soviet invasion. The goal of Bin Laden's acts is to create a pan-Islamic Caliphate throughout the world. To achieve this goal, Bin Laden is working with Islamic extremist groups to overthrow non–Islamic regimes and to force out Westerners and non-Muslims from Islamic countries. Moreover, in 1998, he issued a religious statement (fatwa) saying that all Muslims should kill American citizens—civilian or military—and their allies everywhere. This statement was published under the banner of the "World Islamic Front for Jihad against the Jews and Crusaders" (U.S. Department of State, April 2001).

The case of Al Qaeda and Osama Bin Laden motivates one to legitimately ask many questions. For example, what is terrorism? What is the relationship between religion and terrorism, and what role can religious leaders play in this relationship? In other words, why do some people commit terrorism in the name of religion, and what role can religious leaders play in this kind of violence? What is the relationship between terrorism and religion from the perspective of religious leaders? Is religious-based terrorism limited to Islam? How about other religions such as Judaism and Christianity?

"Terrorism" is an expression that we hear daily. It is used to describe some violent incidents occurring anywhere in the world. It is a type of violence that targets victims from any part of society. Targets of terrorism represent a range of victims including leaders of countries, civilians, military personnel, and even babies in daycares. No one is safe from being a target or a victim of terrorism. This type of violence can happen anytime, anyplace, and against anyone. Therefore, dealing with this violence needs a different approach than that employed to deal with traditional crime; for terrorists have different motives, tactics, and explanations for their violent acts. In addition, terrorism has been labeled as the "international curse" of the twentieth century, and it can continue to be thus for the next decades. Unfortunately, both governments and citizens have to accept this problem as "one of those hazards of life that is not completely resolvable" (Schechterman and Slann, 1998, p. iv). Simply put, terrorism is a global plague, and many countries have suffered, to some extent, from this problem, including the United States.

There are two major types of terrorism: international and domestic. For many Americans, international terrorism is a fairly well-known topic due to the loss of many American lives in several terrorist incidents in the Middle East, Europe, and other places worldwide. In the domestic arena, on the other hand, several terrorist acts have served as a "wake-up call" for the problem of terrorism on American soil. These acts include the destruction of the World

Trade Center in New York and the attack on the Pentagon on September 11, 2001, the 1995 bombing of the Murrah Federal Building in Oklahoma City, the 1993 bombing of the World Trade Center, and the bombing of several abortion clinics in different places in the United States.

Although terrorism is a form of criminal behavior, it is different from other crimes because terrorists commit their crimes, in most cases, for non-personal reasons using different methods to cover their violent acts. Terrorists call themselves many names but not "terrorists." For example, they consider themselves "urban guerrillas," "warriors," "fighters for freedom," and "saviors," to name a few, but most countries do not recognize these names and deal with terrorists as criminals. Finally, terrorists commit their violent acts for many reasons, one of which is committing illegal acts in the name of religion to achieve religious goals.

During the last three decades, terrorism motivated by religion has become a worldwide menace. Almost 20 percent of the fifty well-known worldwide active terrorist groups are identified as having religion as an important factor in their activities (Hoffman, 1995). For these groups, "religion serves as a legitimizing force—conveyed by sacred text or imparted via clerical authorities claiming to speak for the divine" (Hoffman, 1995, p. 272).

However, exploiting religion to legitimize terrorism is not limited to a single religion; it exists in other major religions (e.g., Judaism, Christianity, and Islam). The United States has suffered from religious-based terrorism through numerous remarkable terrorist acts within and outside of American soil. Terrorist incidents, such as the bombing of the World Trade Center and the 1995 Oklahoma City bombing, provide evidence of the problem of religion motivated terrorism on the American domestic level. Other incidents, such as the attacks against American targets in Africa, Saudi Arabia in 1995 and 1996, and the attacks against Americans in Beirut, Lebanon, in the 1980s, represent evidence for the problem of religious-based terrorism facing Americans outside the United States.

The nature of religious-based terrorism is different from other kinds of terrorism. Some see terrorism in the name of religion to be "unprecedented, not only in its scope and the selection of targets, but also in its lethality and indiscriminate character" (Ranstorp, 1996, p. 43). The number of the killed victims in such terrorism is relatively large.

Terrorist acts such as bombing office buildings and embassies, as well as suicide bombers on busy streets, cost the loss of many more innocent lives than any other kinds of traditional crimes or other types of terrorism. The most important aspect of this kind of violence is the fact that the perpetrators believe that they are on a divine mission, that is, they claim that they are executing God's orders. They look for ways to "please" God according to their religion, and they are not looking for immediate or short-term benefits but for God's rewards. Religion and terrorism, hence, have a special relationship. Investigating and understanding this relationship from the perspective of some religious leaders is the cornerstone of this study.

RESEARCH QUESTIONS

Three major research questions provide a framework for organizing the book. They are:

1. How does the perception of terrorism differ between leaders of diverse religions: Judaism, Christianity, and Islam? Do various religious leaders define terrorism differently?

2. What are the attitudes and perceptions of religious leaders regarding the justification of selected terrorist acts?

3. What are the perceptions and attitudes of religious leaders that may promote or discourage selected terrorist acts? That is, what specific roles might be played by religious leaders to reduce or promote terrorist activity?

In short, the three research questions are focused on the areas of defining terrorism, justifying religious-based terrorism, and dealing with this kind of violence.

Significance of the Problem

"The extent to which religion plays a role [in motivating terrorism] remains a puzzle, even among experts" (Kidder, 1993, p. 30). Religion and terrorism share a long history. In fact, the roots of some words that describe terrorists and their violent acts in the English language (e.g., thug, zealot, and assassin) can be traced back to religious terrorist groups active in previous eras (Hoffman, 1995).

Despite the history and the wide scope of the problem of terrorism, it is still under-represented in the scientific and academic literature. Historians, journalists, military and intelligence analysts, political scientists, and others have written the literature on terrorism, not academic criminologists or practitioners in criminal justice (Martin, 1988). This statement appears basically true and valid today in the field of criminology, which has the least share in the literature on terrorism. A search of major journals and textbooks in the field of criminology and criminal justice clarifies this point with very few pages and articles found on this topic.

In other words, despite the huge number of publications about terrorism in the literature, the need for specialized scientific research in this area is still massive. There are thousands of published books and articles available on terrorism (Shukry, 1991). Yet the lack of scholarly research on terrorism stands out because most of the information on this topic comes from journalistic media resources, and, in some cases, from government agency official records and reports (Smith and Morgan, 1996). Therefore, a systematic research in this kind of violence is crucial, timely, and needed for the field of criminology.

The need for a better understanding of the relationship between terrorism and religion is as great as ever. In the midst of television's news headlines, movies, and the huge number of pages in print journalism about events and acts of terrorism, the temptation remains to view terrorism as associated with religion. Hence, a thorough scientific inquiry can shed light on the truth of the complex relationship between religion and terrorism.

Many Americans, and other people in the world, rely on media and politicians to formulate their own ideas about terrorism. In 2001, after the terrible terrorist attacks in the United States, the focus of media was on Muslims and the Middle East as a logical source of the apparent terrorist acts. Before that, however, after the Oklahoma City bombing in 1995, the Middle East was initially suspected. Although Islam is not the only religion inspiring terrorism in its name, it is the religion most often linked to terrorism in the American media. Clearly, individuals and/or groups commit terrorism in the name of other religions, which include Judaism and Christianity as well.

In short, each religion has its own terrorists and extremists. Because of this distinction, this book is critically necessary in order to understand, in a systematic way, the complex relationship between religion and terrorism not only in Islam but also in the other two monotheistic religions, Judaism and Christianity.
A further significance of this study lies in taking religion as a cause (independent variable) for promoting terrorism (dependent variable), not the reverse. It has been noticed that religion plays an important role, or is considered as a social bond in preventing people from engaging in criminal behavior.

E. Durkheim investigated the relationship between religion and suicide (a crime at that time) and found that the suicide rate is low in societies where religion plays an important role in integrating people (1897, 1951). In other words, the high degree of social integration associated with religion discourages people from committing criminal behavior (i.e., there is an inverse relationship between criminal behavior and religion). Based on this inverse relationship between religion and criminal behavior, some prisons use religion in their rehabilitation programs in an attempt to control inmates' future criminal behaviors.

This book investigates a reverse relationship between religion and criminal behavior (terrorism). That is, how might religion become a motive for criminal behavior in the specific case of terrorism? For example, many suicide bombers were motivated by religious beliefs to commit their acts. Therefore, this kind of behavior represents a new menace to society and the criminal justice system. The terrorist in this case "is not just prepared to get killed, he wants to get killed" (Kidder, 1993, p. 32).

In addition, this study is significant since it addresses terrorism in the three monotheistic religions (Judaism, Christianity, and Islam) and tries to reach individual (for each religion) and total (for the three religions combined) understanding of religious-based terrorism. In other words, it seeks to develop an inter-religion or inter-faith investigation of the problem of terrorism. Therefore, this study goes beyond the individual and strict explanations within each religion, and explores points of agreements and disagreements among the three religions in explaining terrorist violence.

This book investigates inter- and intra-religious-based terrorism, that is, terrorism by and among people within each of the three religions, and terrorism against people of other religions. From this perspective, a goal of this study has been to gather needed social science evidence to add to the growing but deficient body of literature on terrorism, particularly on religious-based terrorism. Furthermore, the results of this study may help policymakers and citizens of the United States and/or other countries in their efforts to manage this type of illegal behavior (terrorism).

Chapter 2

General Information on Religion

The purpose of this part is to introduce the reader to the first of two complex topics: religion and terrorism. The nature and importance of religion cannot be underrated when discussing terrorism. To this end, this part will include the following sections:

    a. Religion, and definitions of the terms related to it (i.e., religion: Judaism, Christianity, and Islam; religious leaders: rabbis, priests, and Imams/Sheikhs).
    b. Terrorism (definitions, types, terrorism in the United States).
    c. Religion and terrorism (Judaism, Christianity, Islam, and terrorism).
    d. Research and the problems of doing research on terrorism.

RELIGION

Discussing detailed origins, beliefs, or similarities and differences among the religions involved in this book is beyond its scope. However, in this section an overview of religion, and definitions of some terms related to it, is necessary to acquaint the reader with this topic.

Religion is an interdisciplinary field. Each social science studies religions from different angles. Archaeology, for example, focuses on the prehistoric times of human life, and evidence of religious rituals is an important clue to ancient society; anthropology and sociology study the role of religion in societies; and psychology focuses on the impact of religion on the individual's behavior. Universities throughout the world offer special programs (graduate and undergraduate) and degrees in religious studies.

Thus, religion is a broad field, and this researcher does not claim any specialty in this discipline. However, since the interest of this book is in the social importance of religion in society, and how religion becomes a motive for illegal behavior (in this case terrorism), a brief overview of this topic is needed.

Religion is a universal phenomenon that plays an important role in the life of any society. This role has been noticed since the beginning of human life.

In his book, *The Elementary Forms of Religious Life*, E. Durkheim explored the question of why religion is universal in human societies (1912, 1965, cited in Martin, et al 1990). He found that religion is a social fact and not simply the product of the psychology of certain individuals. Religion cannot be considered to be an illusion because it appears in every age in all parts of the world, and great cultures and systems of morality and law were based on religion. Durkheim also noted that religion helps to maintain society, but he concluded that groups, in fact, worship society itself. Religion creates a moral community and as such solidarity of the society is enhanced. As a result, religion serves the goal of promoting order and unity in society (Durkheim, 1912, cf., in Martin, Mutchnick, and Austin, 1990; Eitzen and Zinn, 1988; Parrinder, 1971).

For a group that shares the same religious heritage and beliefs, three positive consequences are expected: unity, social control, and the legitimization of social structure (Etzen and Zinn, 1988, pp. 523-524). For the purposes of unity, all believers of a religion, regardless of their demographic differences, are "united through the sharing of the same system of beliefs" (Eitzen and Zinn, 1988). Religion, "provides them with values to be followed, sins to be avoided, and rules to be implemented." Group unity also occurs through the feeling that God looks upon them or the notion that "God is on our side" (Eitzen and Zinn, 1988, p.522). An example of this feeling is found in a verse of the national anthem of Great Britain:

> O Lord our God, arise
> Scatter our enemies
> And make them fall.
> Confound their politics,
> Frustrate their knavish tricks,
> On thee our hopes we fix,
> God save us all. (cited in Eitzen and Zinn, 1988, p. 523)

Lately, an upsurge in the popularity of the American song "God Bless America" further illustrates this point.

The second positive consequence of religion is providing social control in society (Eitzen and Zinn, 1988). This goal is accomplished in two ways. First, there are certain punishments for any violation of the explicit rules that religion provides. Second, children internalize the religious beliefs by socializing with other children and with adults. The rules that children learn in order to be accepted members of society work through the feeling of guilt and/or fear of breaking the rules.

The final positive consequence of religion is the legitimization of social structure. Religion provides blessing to the values and institutions of society. In American society, for example, private property and free enterprise have become almost sacred. Many people also believe that "democracy" is one of God's orders (Eitzen and Zinn, 1988).

Although religion promotes group integration, it may also divide society and its groups (Eitzen and Zinn, 1988). Many religious groups tend to focus on separateness and superiority by defining others as inferior (e.g., terms such as "infidels," "heathens," "heretics," or "nonbelievers" are often used to describe others). This separation happens because each religious group feels that it has the way, and sometimes the only way, to reach salvation or any other religious goals. This could happen not only between people or societies from different religions, but also within groups from the same religion, and even within the same religious sect. As a result, conflict between religious groups (inter-and intra-conflict) has been noticed all over the world. For example, there are religious conflicts between Christians and Muslims in the Philippines (Austin, in press; 1991; 1989); Jews and Muslims in the Middle East; Catholic and Protestant in Northern Ireland, and other conflicts in Europe and the United States. Thus, religious conflict is a global problem and it has a big impact on American interests all over the world (Shultz and Schmauder, 1994).

Religion takes different forms of belief around the world. The belief in a god is primary to most religious dogma. This belief is described in the literature with the term "theism." On the other hand, belief in one god is called "monotheism" (Parrinder, 1971). Monotheism appears in three major religions, Judaism, Christianity, and Islam, which is the focus of this study.

Judaism

Judaism is the religion of Jewish people. According to this religion, after the Exodus of the Hebrews from Egypt, God gave Moses a divine revelation, and ordered him and his people (the Hebrews) to make a commitment to God's will. There is a close connection between religion and citizenry in Judaism, giving this religion a special position among other religions. This unique position makes it hard to separate the long history of Judaism from the history of Jews, which goes back more than 3,000 years (Corbett, 1994; Parrinder, 1971).

The Jewish belief is based on the recognition of one eternal God who created the universe, and who is the master of every aspect of this universe. God also created human beings and gave them the ability to choose between good and evil. Human beings can communicate with God through prayers and meditation. Through revelation, God has given people the Torah (the Divine Law) by which they can establish God's kingdom on earth. This kingdom will be recognized by the arrival of a personal Messiah, who will be human and descended from the house of David. Jewish people believe that they have a special role in this divine scheme because God revealed the Torah to them via Moses on Mount Sinai. Obedience to the Torah is a very serious element in Judaism, which is enacted through fulfillment of the Commandments, composed of 248 positive and 365 negative regulatory principles (Corbett, 1994; Parrinder, 1971).

Judaism is classified under three major divisions: Orthodox, Reform, and Conservative. Orthodox Judaism is a sect representing traditional Judaism.

Jews in this sect literally believe in the revelation at Sinai as written in the Torah. They accept the written and oral law as divine, and they also accept the authority of rabbis, the experts in the Talmud. Although this sect, in general, is united around certain beliefs, some differences are found in belief and ceremony. Finally, the label "Orthodox" originally was not a Jewish name. It was borrowed from Christianity and was used to describe rigid traditionalism (i.e., fundamentalism) by Reform Jews.

Reform Judaism refers to another Jewish sect. In 1818, a group of Jews in Hamburg, Germany, built a synagogue which they called a temple. They used German in their prayer, shortened the service, and introduced to Judaism some modern ideas. Some of their new ideas are; confirmation for boys and girls in place of the traditional Bar Mitzvah; giving up the belief in a personal Messiah; and the insistence that the land of Jews is where they reside (home), not the land of Israel. These Jews also eliminated head covering, dietary restrictions, and other laws that they considered outdated. This sect emphasized ethical elements over ritual. Reform Jews inspired a strong opposition from the traditional Jews, and there is an ongoing debate between them and other sects about who exactly are the true representatives of Judaism.

The third sect of Judaism is the Conservative Jew. This sect arose in the United States in the late nineteenth and the early twentieth centuries. The founders of this movement opposed the Reform sect; they focused on the importance of the Jewish nationhood, the land of Israel, and the Hebrew language. Like other sects in Judaism, Conservative groups have some tensions among them over issues of theology, religious practice, and the place of women in the rabbinate (Corbett, 1994; Parrinder, 1971).

Christianity

Christian belief is focused on one God revealed to the world through Jesus of Nazareth who lived as a human being for about thirty years in Palestine. The Romans crucified Jesus at Jerusalem at the beginning of the first century. Christians believe that Jesus rose from the dead after three days and his disciples saw him on numerous occasions during the succeeding forty days. Central to this religion is the doctrine that Christians do not worship a dead person; rather they believe in the living Christ. Christianity is one of the major religions in the world, and Christians form about two-sevenths of the world's population. Christians are divided into three main categories: Roman Catholic, Protestant, and Eastern Orthodox. However, there are other Christian groups who do not fall within any of these three categories (Corbett, 1994; Parrinder, 1971).

Regardless of any differences, Christian groups, in general, share certain elements that define them under the rubric of Christianity. These elements include: (a) the belief that Jesus Christ is the second person in the Trinity of God the Father, the Son, and the Holy Spirit; (b) the use of sacred rites; reverence for the Old and New Testaments as authoritative Holy Scripture; (c) the requirement of a morally disciplined life; and (d) the maintenance of a structure of church government and the body of trained clergy (Corbett, 1994).

Christian belief in God has a unique character, which is the concept of the fatherhood of God. According to this religion God is the "Father Almighty," and the "maker of heaven and earth." Christians' belief in Christ, on the other hand, is an important step in this religion, and it is the main factor that differentiates Christianity from the other two monotheistic religions (Judaism and Islam). Christ, for Christians, is the "Son of God" and "Lord and Savior." His birth was of the Virgin Mary. Thus, Christ had "two natures in one person"; he was divine and human at the same time. Another major element in Christianity is the belief in the Holy Spirit. This element has inspired different interpretations among Christians, some of which (Eastern Church) regarded the Holy Spirit as a creature like the angels, and the Spirit "proceeds from the Father." In the West, following St. Augustine's view, the phrase "and the Son" was inserted after "proceeds from the Father" in liturgical texts. The Eastern Church considered this modification to be very offensive. So Protestantism and Roman Catholicism agree on this element and both of them disagree with Eastern Orthodoxy in explaining the concept of the Holy Spirit. Nevertheless, in the twentieth century the issue of how the Holy Spirit proceeds from the Father and the Son came under discussion by Roman Catholic and Eastern Orthodox theologians (Corbett, 1994; Parrinder, 1971).

Islam

Islam is an Arabic word that denotes submission, surrender, and obedience; the other literal meaning of the word is peace. As a religion, Islam stands for complete submission and obedience to Allah (the one and the only God).

Muslims are those people who believe in Islam as a religion and a way of life. A person may become a Muslim simply by believing that there is no God but Allah and that Muhammed, Peace Be Upon Him (PBUH), is his messenger. More than one billion people are Muslims, representing a wide range of races, nationalities, and cultures from all over the world. Only about 18 percent of Muslims live in the Arab world. Indonesia is the largest Muslim country in the world. In the United States, approximately five million people follow the religion of Islam. Almost half of the Muslim population in the United States are African Americans, many of whom follow a sect called the "Nation of Islam" which bases its belief on racial issues. The second half consists of Muslims from other places of origin, mostly Asian countries. The number of Muslim Arabs in the United States is low compared to other groups. Eventually, Islam is expected to be the second major religion in America after Christianity (Mazrui, 1996).

Muslims believe in one, unique, and incomparable God; in the angels; in the prophets; in the Day of Judgment and in life after death; and in God's indisputable authority over human destiny. Individuals, according to Islam, are responsible for their actions, and God will ask them about their deeds during their lifetimes. Further, Muslims believe in all the prophets who were sent before Muhammed (PBUH) starting from Adam and including Noah, Abraham, Ishmael, Isaac, Jacob, Joseph, Moses, David, Solomon, and Jesus (PBUT).

However, Muslims believe that God's final message to humankind was revealed to the Prophet Muhammed (PBUH) through the Angel Gabriel, and that there is no prophet after him (Sabig, 1984).

Judaism, Christianity, and Islam share the same root. Their prophets came from the same father: Abraham, Moses, and Jesus (Peace Be Upon Them) descended from Abraham's son Isaac, and Muhammed from Abraham's eldest son Ishmael (PBUT). Abraham built the old house, Ka'ba, in what is today the city of Makkah, four thousand years ago. God ordered Abraham and Ishmael to build this place. Ka'ba is the place toward which all Muslims face five times a day when they pray (Parrinder, 1971).

There are two major sects in Islam that arose after the death of the Prophet (PBUH): Sunnah or Sunni (the majority, approximately 90 percent) and Shia (the minority, 10 to 15 percent); but there are other subdivisions within each category. Sunni or Sunnah represents the traditional sect of Islam. They believe in the Quran and Hadith, and they respect and follow the traditions of the four caliphs who succeeded the Prophet (PBUH). They also recognize and obey any good Muslim as the ruler of the Islamic state regardless of his origin, family, or any other personal facts.

Shia, as groups, have appeared after disagreements regarding leadership of Muslim states and communities. They put conditions for the head of state. These included descent from Ali's sons (Ali is the cousin and son-in-law of the Prophet). They maintained some reservations against the leadership of the first three caliphs because the Shia favored the rule of Ali over the others.

Shia believe in a series of Imams who are from Ali's family (particularly from his sons) for leadership of the Muslims. The largest group of the Shiites, the Twelvers, recognize twelve Imams, the last of whom disappeared and who will return to rule the Islamic nation. In general, Shiites follow the same doctrine and practice of Islam as do other Muslims. The Shia hold major differences with Sunni which include belief concerning the Imam and other legal aspects in Islam. The largest state of Shia is Iran, but they are scattered throughout most of the Islamic countries and communities (Sabig, 1984).

DEFINITIONS OF TERMS RELATED TO RELIGION

For purposes of this book, the following definitions will be used for terms and concepts related to the three religions under study.

Religious-based Terrorism

Religious-based terrorism is any use, or threat of use, of violence of a criminal nature against innocent victims or property by a religious group, organization, state, or individual for religious/political reasons against targets within that religion or targets from other religions.

Rabbi

The word "rabbi" means "my teacher." A rabbi has the authority to preach the Jewish scriptural and oral traditions of the Old Testament or Torah. According to Orthodox Judaism, a rabbi must be a male, whereas in the other two sects, Reform and Conservative Judaism, gender is not an issue. For the purposes of this study, rabbi will be defined as any individual who leads Jewish prayers and gives orations, or speeches, or preaches in a synagogue, whether as a part-time or full-time employee or a volunteer.

Priest

In this study, the term "priest" will pertain to one who has the authority to preach in a Christian church and to interpret Christian doctrines as derived from the Bible. The word "priest" is often reserved for Catholic leaders. Some Protestant leaders hold the title of priest (such as Episcopal), but many use the title of minister or preacher.

Imam and/or Sheikh

The two titles will be used interchangeably in this study. Imam or sheikh can be defined as a person who holds authority similar to the priest and rabbi but officiates in a Muslim mosque. In Islam, only males can lead prayer and preach in mosques. Moreover, "sheikh" is a title used for a religious person especially who works in a mosque. "Imam," on the other hand, is a title for he who leads prayers and gives Friday's speech. Nevertheless, "sheikh" and "Imam" have other meanings. The word "sheikh" can be used as a label for a head of a tribe in the Arab culture; for a member of a ruling family (as in Kuwait and other Gulf states, for example), or for a religious person who performs religious duties. The word "Imam" always has a religious meaning, referring either to a regular person performing as a religious leader, or to the Imam, according to Shia, who belongs to Ali's family (Prophet Muhammad's cousin and son-in-law).

Chapter 3

Terrorism: Selective Literature Review

Reviewing the literature on terrorism is not an easy task. Terrorism is an interdisciplinary topic involving different fields, for example, sociology, psychology, economics, communications, and political science. Surprisingly, based on available publications, criminology has the least share in dealing with this kind of violence. For example, looking at the American Society of Criminology (ASC) and Academy of Criminal Justice Sciences (ACJS) conferences and programs, one finds only a few sessions on the topic. Until recently, one could not find any paper or roundtable discussion on terrorism in these organizations' annual conferences. Moreover, criminology and criminal justice journals reflected scant research on this topic until after the Oklahoma City bombing. Some criminologists discussed terrorism as part of political crimes (e.g., Friedlander, 1979). Lately, with heightened interest since September 11, terrorism became a new topic in most criminology and criminal justice textbooks, although with limited depth or scope.

Keeping in mind the general lack of criminological and scientific literature on terrorism, and on religious-based terrorism in particular, a selective information review will be presented here. This review is divided into five subtopics: definition of terrorism, types of terrorism, differences between terrorism and traditional crimes, terrorism in the United States, and counterterrorism.

DEFINING TERRORISM

It is very rare to read any publication about terrorism without noticing the difficulty of defining terrorism. Defining terrorism is a major problem for researchers and law enforcement agencies. Terrorists call themselves many names: urban guerrillas, warriors, or freedom fighters (Revell, 1987).

There is an ongoing discussion about how to define terrorism. Implicit in this debate is the assumption that it may be in the "eye of the beholder." B. Schechterman and M. Slann (1998) employ two approaches in defining terrorism: the "minimalist" and the "maximalist." The first approach focuses on three elements: perpetrators, victims, and audiences affected by terrorist acts. The victim element is the one that creates extensive debates. For the United States, a noncombatant victim is evident in the definition of a terrorist act. The maximalist approach, on the other hand, favored by the Israelis and others, recognizess the civilian victim as a major element in a terrorist act, but it adds passive military targets to be considered as civilian victims in defining a terrorist act. Thus, defining terrorism is important not only regarding what acts can be considered terrorist, but also for the sake of how to deal with terrorism.

In the literature, there are over one hundred definitions of terrorism, and yet there appears to be no single accepted definition (Schmid, 1983). Nevertheless, Schmid outlined twenty-two elements in these definitions, and developed a consensus definition consisting of five parts. First, terrorism is a method of combat in which random or symbolic victims are targets of violence. Second, through previous use of violence or the credible threat of violence, other members of that group or class are put in a state of chronic fear. Third, the victimization of the target is considered beyond the norm by most observers. Fourth, this victimization creates an audience beyond the target of terror. Fifth, the purpose of terrorism is either to immobilize the target of terror in order to produce disorientation and/or compliance, or to mobilize secondary targets of attention, for example, public opinion (Gurr, 1988; Sederberg, 1991). Despite Schmid's effort in defining terrorism, he neglects terrorist acts against property.

In addition, J. Gibbs (1989) provides a definition of terrorism that deviates somewhat from the norm. He maintains that terrorism can be defined as any illegal violence or threat of violence directed against human or nonhuman objects. Gibbs postulates that this act has to be governed by a number of factors that determine it as an act of terrorism. First, the act should be undertaken, or ordered, with the intention of changing or maintaining at least one putative norm in at least one particular geographical or demographic unit. Second, the incident has to be characterized as covert and furtive to facilitate the concealment of the perpetrators' identification or location. Third, the terrorist activity is not undertaken or planned to support the permanent defense of some area. Fourth, terrorism is not a conventional warfare; because of the terrorists' concealment tactics of identity and location which cannot be classified under the rubrics of conventional military standards. Fifth, the violent act is perceived by the perpetrators as a contribution in the normative end, previously described, by planting fear of violence in persons other than the immediate, actual, or threatened target.

The problem in defining terrorism is not limited to the academic and research community. The criminal justice community faces the same problem. A number of different federal agencies in the United States have their own definition of terrorism (State Department, Defense Department, Department of

Justice, etc., so presenting and discussing these definitions is beyond the scope of this section). However, the FBI, the leading agency in dealing with terrorism, defines terrorism as follows:

Terrorism is the unlawful use of force or violence against persons or property to intimidate or coerce a government, the civilian population, or any segment thereof, in furtherance of political or social objectives. (FBI, 1993)

Although a good effort was made in formulating these definitions, still they do not include terrorism motivated by religion. This brief overview of the problem of defining terrorism provides a legitimate ground for the first research question of this study which is defining terrorism from the religious leaders' perspective.

TYPES OF TERRORISM

Two major types of terrorism are identified in the literature: international and domestic. Groups that operate on disregard of national borders commit international terrorism, which is, in some cases, supported by individual nations. Objectives of international terrorism include attraction of international attention, harm to the relationships of the target country with other countries, and damage to the economy and public order in the target country (Ezeldin, 1990).

Native groups or individuals within the boundaries of a single country, on the other hand, commit domestic terrorism. This type of terrorism seeks to achieve certain goals, among them: (a) to make a political statement; (b) to show the inability of the government to maintain the security of society; (c) to cause physical damage to police, army, or security forces; (d) to change the political system; and (e) to attack government buildings and/or other targets to weaken the government (Ezeldin, 1990).

Terrorists use different tactics in committing terrorist acts. These tactics include, but are not limited to, arson, assassination, hijacking, hostage taking, kidnapping, and bombing. Bombing appears to be the most popular method; it is destructive and relatively easy to carry out. The 1993 bombing of the World Trade Center in New York, the 1995 bombing of the federal building in Oklahoma City, and the 1996 bombing of American buildings in Saudi Arabia are examples of this kind of tactic. Although these tactics seem like traditional crimes, terrorism is different.

TERRORISM VERSUS TRADITIONAL CRIME

There are major differences between terrorists and traditional criminals. Traditional criminals try to achieve personal goals. The primary goal is to acquire money or material goods, or to kill or injure a specific victim (i.e., personal interest). In other words, traditional crime is not designed to have any results beyond the scope of the act itself. The traditional criminals are not interested in attracting public opinion, whereas terrorists want to win the support of public opinion and are looking for benefits and effects beyond the terrorist act. Most terrorists want to change the system (or some elements in the system) but criminals do not. Finally, terrorists often do not consider themselves terrorists, but argue that society and law enforcement personnel are the terrorists (Kellen, 1982).

Despite the fact that terrorists may use traditional crimes in their activities, it is not the crimes themselves that distinguish terrorists from traditional criminals. It is their views of crimes as means to achieve certain goals that make the difference (Kellen, 1982). In a democratic society, there are many peaceful means that citizens can use to achieve their goals: elections, petitions, antigovernment marches, and demonstrations (Yerushalmi, 1987). However, terrorists do not believe in peaceful means. They perceive violence as the best means to achieve their goals (Laqueur, 1996).

TERRORISM IN THE UNITED STATES

Until the September 11, 2001 attack on the World Trade Center and the Pentagon, most Americans were only familiar with terrorism as something that happens outside of the United States. Even after the 1993 bombing of the World Trade Center, the problem of terrorism inside the country was still unfamiliar to many (Perry, 1997). Terrorist acts against American targets in the Middle East, Europe, and other places are not unknown to most Americans (e.g., the 1979 hostage crises in the American embassy in Iran; attacks against U.S. Marines in Lebanon in 1983; the bombing of Pan American Flight 103 over Lockerbie, Scotland; and the bombing of the American military compound in Saudi Arabia in 1996). Even in the wake of the September 11 bombings, the problem of terrorism within the United States (domestic terrorism) is subject to much misinformation and guesswork.

Until September 11, 2001, both ordinary people in the United States and law enforcement agencies were largely unfamiliar with domestic terrorism. After a presentation to a group of more than one hundred law enforcement officers (patrol officers, investigators, supervisors, and chiefs), most were astonished to learn of the breadth of the problem of domestic terrorism (Mullins, 1988). American police and security agencies "literally do not know what terrorism is," and agencies that deal with countering terrorism are not aware of or are clueless in dealing with this problem (White 1991). Unfortunately, terrorism does exist in the United States. In 1988, more than 150 terrorist organizations were active within the United States (Mullins). Many of them represent a small number of members, while others pretend to have thousands of members (for example, the Ku Klux Klan and Aryan Nations). Hence, the United States, like any other country in this world, suffers the problem of domestic terrorism, and as B. Hoffman (1988) claims, the United States is no longer immune from terrorism within its own borders.

There is no specific classification for terrorists within the United States. J. White (1991) suggests five major categories. These include revolutionary nationalists, the ideological right, the ideological left, criminal groups using terrorist acts, and foreign groups operating in America. Similarly, one researcher points out five categories of terrorism but with different names: Puerto Rican leftist, black militants, right-wing extremists, and Jewish extremists (Harris, 1987). Other researchers classify terrorist groups in three categories of left-wing, right-wing, and single-issue terrorism (Revell, 1987; Stinson 1987; Albanese, 1993).

Terrorist Groups in the United States

There is no universally accepted classification of terrorist groups in the United States. However, this study will adopt the following classifications: left-wing, right-wing, special-issue, and international group terrorism.

Left-Wing Terrorism
During the post-Vietnam War era of the early 1970s, attacks of the left wing focused on symbols of American imperialism and what these groups saw as capitalistic exploitation of Third World nations by the United States. Their targets included banks, corporate offices, and military facilities, which were chosen to publicize their cause and existence. Operations were staged to generate what these left-wing terrorists refer to as "armed propaganda" (Revell, 1987; Stinson, 1987). Left-wing terrorism has been cyclical. There have been periods of terrorist violence followed by arrests and prosecutions, followed by a regrouping stage of the terrorist group. The left–wing groups currently appears to be in a regrouping stage (Albanese, 1993). In short, left-wing terrorism hopes "to change a government to socialism, communism, or anarchism" (Mullins, 1997, p. 33).

Right-Wing Terrorism
Most right-wing terrorist organizations have a Christian ideology in their agenda. Therefore, more details will be presented on this type in the special section on Christianity and terrorism. However, examples from this wing include the following organizations: The Aryan Nations, The Order, The Sword, The Arm of the Lord, and the Ku Klux Klan (KKK). The basic beliefs of the far-right-wing organizations include the power of the white race and the hate of non-white people. Right-wing terrorism is based upon ideologies of racial or religious supremacy (Kaplan, 1997; Schechterman and Slann, 1998).

Special-Issue Terrorism
Between and often beyond left- and right-wing terrorism, one can place the "special-issue" terrorism. It has different ideologies and goals and focuses on some particular elements of society and environment. Terrorists in this category

look for specific change in policies, laws, or programs (Eagan, 1996). The FBI and the criminal justice system consider anti-abortionist forces, the animal-rights-oriented "Animal Liberation Front" (ALF), and the Eco-Terrorists to be the most recent groups employing terrorist tactics for special purposes and issues (FBI, 1993). A number of bombings and acts of vandalism directed at abortion clinics or pro-abortion centers have occurred throughout the U.S. Also, the ALF has used arson, vandalism, and theft against animal research laboratories (Albanese, 1993).

International Terrorist Groups
The capability of the international groups to commit terrorism within the United States is not yet fully known. The following groups have conducted terrorist operations, or have active members in the United States: Armenian Secret Army for the Liberation of Armenia (ASALA), Indian Sikh, Libyan Network, Palestinian groups, Northern Ireland groups, Iranian groups (Stinson, 1987), and some Islamic like-minded groups and individuals such as the group convicted of the 1993 bombing of the World Trade Center (WTC) in New York. Foreign terrorists are thought to be living in the United States, and they are awaiting the signal from their sponsors to launch their terrorist acts (Mullins,1997). The FBI keeps special lists of most international students "who fit the demographic profile of the terrorists" (p. 41).

COUNTERING TERRORISM

Terrorism is a complicated topic, and it is a real problem for Americans within and outside the United States. Understanding it is the first step in dealing with this problem. The September 11, 2001 attack and the 1995 Oklahoma City and 1993 World Trade Center bombings are signs of this problem inside the United States. Therefore, it is necessary to understand this problem and the message that terrorists try to send to society and the government before making plans to counter it. The terrorists' message to the target government is "no matter how small we are, no matter how big and powerful you are, we can hurt you if you do not do what we want" (Cetron, 1989).

Most governments are still studying the message of terrorists and trying to find the right response. There is no one solution for the problem of terrorism, and most policies dealing with it are still far from achieving significant results (Shultz and Schmauder, 1994). J. Albanese (1993), on the other hand, argues that countering terrorism takes three stages.

The first stage is the "ideal stage," that is, before a terrorist act occurs. At this stage, governments and law enforcement agencies may take several steps to prevent terrorist attacks. These include promoting security precautions in sensitive places, such as airports and government targets, conducting effective intelligence operations to collect information that prevent potential terrorist acts, and minimizing public support for terrorist groups.

The second stage starts when the ideal stage fails. At the second stage, different activities are needed to deal with a terrorist act such as negotiating with terrorists, minimizing the damage of a terrorist act, and preventing public panic during and after a terrorist act.

The third stage deals with terrorists after a terrorist act, when an act is successfully completed, and when the terrorist has fled the scene. Here the law enforcement effort is to apprehend, prosecute, and if convicted, punish the terrorist (Albanese, 1993).

The United States counters terrorism with political and legal means. The American official policy in dealing with terrorism is based on the following four steps: first, make no concession to terrorists and strike no deals; second, bring terrorists to justice for their crimes; third, isolate and apply pressure on states that sponsor terrorism to force them to change their behavior; fourth, bolster the counterterrorist capabilities of those countries that work with the United States and require assistance (U.S. Dept. of State, April 2001).

On the legal front, the U.S. government has passed a special law to counter terrorism. The Anti-Terrorism Act of 1996 is the current implemented federal law to punish terrorists. Before this act, terrorism was viewed in two different ways, as international terrorism and domestic terrorism. In the international arena, specific laws were available. However, domestic terrorism was considered and dealt with as a traditional crime. To fill this gap, the 1996 law classified terrorism as a federal crime and had enhanced the penalty for convicted terrorists to include the death penalty or life in prison (Anti-Terrorism Act of PL-104-132-1996).

Distinguishing between terrorism and other violent acts is not an easy task. It depends on where one stands in looking at and defining terrorism. Terrorists do not necessarily accept the label of terrorism. They call themselves many names: urban guerrillas, warriors, or freedom fighters (Revell, 1987). Most researchers agree with the two designations of terrorism as international terrorism and domestic terrorism (e.g., Albanese, 1993; Ezeldin, 1990; Kupperman, 1986). International terrorism has become a familiar issue to most Americans (Albanese, 1993). However, until recently, domestic terrorism was less known than international terrorism. Over a decade ago, 150 terrorist organizations who formed the basis for domestic terrorism were active within the United States (Mullins, 1988). By the mid-1990s the number of terrorist organizations increased to include more than two thousand groups. Some groups have few people, and others have thousands, such as militia groups (Mullins). Domestic terrorism became better known to most Americans after the 1993 bombing of the World Trade Center (WTC), the 1995 bombing of the federal building in Oklahoma City (Eagan, 1996), and the 1996 bombing at the Olympic Games in Atlanta. Since the September 11, 2001 attacks, the existence of domestic terrorism has become quite well known.

It is imperative to say that terrorists fight for different reasons, including political, social, environmental, and religious. Many terrorist groups have used their spiritual ideology to commit violence in the name of religion.

Chapter 4

Religion and Terrorism

Let us look at the two concepts, religion and terrorism, when they work together in the case of religious-based terrorism. In the last two decades, many groups have used their religion to justify, rationalize, and defend their illegal violence, particularly in the case of terrorism. This phenomenon has been named the "holy terror," and it is argued that until the nineteenth century, "religion provided the only acceptable justification for terrorism" (Rapoport, 1984, 1988). This phenomenon has been observed in major religions all over the world (from Japan to the United States, including Europe, India, and the Middle East). The focus of this book is limited to three major religions: Judaism, Christianity, and Islam.

To many Americans, terrorism is violence committed by "radical Muslims" or "crazed anarchists" (Eagan, 1996), but it is now understood that some Christians and Jews have also used religion to justify and legitimate aggression, warfare, violence, and terrorism (Esposito, 1995; Hoffman, 1995; Ranstorp, 1996).

Religion and terrorism share a long history. Many words in the English language that describe terrorism and violence have religious etymology (Hoffman, 1995; Ranstorp, 1996). The word zealot, for example, dates to a Jewish sect in 66–73AD. The word "assassin" comes from an Islamic terrorist group that existed between 1090 and 1272; and the term "thug" derived from an Indian religious group in the seventh century (Hoffman, 1995). In the first half of the twentieth century, religious-based terrorism was "overshadowed by ethnic and nationalist separatist, or ideologically motivated-terrorism" (Hoffman, 1995).

In the last two decades, the problem of religious-based terrorism has surfaced again, and now half of the well-known terrorist organizations use religion as the major motive for their acts (Hoffman, 1997). In 1968 (the year considered the beginning of modern international terrorism), there was no religious terrorist group active among the terrorist organizations. The year 1980 witnessed the first two international religious terrorist groups, but they were just 2 out of 64 terrorist organizations. The number of religious terrorist groups, then, began to increase to become 11 out of 48 in 1992. In 1996, almost half of the active terrorist groups were religious-based terrorists: 25, or 45 percent, of the 58 terrorist organizations (Hoffman, 1997).

It can be concluded that the trend to combine religion with terrorism is approaching the norm at both international and domestic levels. J. Kelly and W. Cook (1995) assert that with religion, no other moral or individual responsibility is required to justify terrorism. By using religion, the morality of terrorism is self-explained. Moreover, B. Hoffman (1995) argues that for some terrorist groups, religion serves as a legitimizing force "conveyed by sacred text or imported via clerical authorities claiming to speak for the divine" (p. 272).

THE THREAT OF RELIGIOUS TERRORISM

As mentioned before, religious-based terrorism is a real threat against America and other countries in the world. It is more lethal than traditional (secular) terrorism, due to the difference in value systems and modes of legitimization. Terrorism in the name of religion is "unprecedented, not only in its scope and the selection of the targets, but also in its lethality and indiscriminate character" (Ranstorp, 1996, p. 43). Under this kind of violence, human rights are severely violated, and respect or consideration of these rights is out of the question (Vyver, 1996). For religious terrorists, violence (or terrorism) is a divine duty, justified by scripture. This explains why religious leaders or figures are, in most cases, required to "bless" (i.e., sanctify, approve) terrorists' acts before they can be undertaken (Hoffman, 1997).

Relying on religious doctrine and/or approval from a religious leader (in any religion) is essential in preparing for a terrorist act. Once that approval has been granted, any kind of violence is acceptable and justified (Holden, 1987; White, 1986). Thus, one may argue that religious leaders can influence the outcome of this kind of violence (religious-based terrorism) in any religion. The next three sections will discuss the relationship between each of the three religions under investigation (Judaism, Christianity, and Islam) and terrorism.

JUDAISM AND TERRORISM

Historical Jewish Terrorism

The first religious terrorist organization appears to have been Jewish. In the first century, a Jewish sect (Zealots-Sicarii) was active in fighting the Roman occupation in Palestine and committed many terrorist acts in the name of Judaism (Laqueur, 1977, 1987; Rapoport, 1984). This sect launched a campaign of individual assassinations and group slaughter, poisoned wells used by Romans, and sabotaged Jerusalem's water supply (Laqueur, 1977, 1987; Rapoport, 1984). Reportedly the violence was religiously motivated.

D. Rapoport states:

The nature of their messianic doctrines simultaneously suggested the object of terror, and permitted methods necessary to achieve it. Jewish apocalyptic prophecies visualize the signs of the imminence of the Messiah as a series of massive catastrophes involving whole populations, the upsetting of all moral order to the point of dissolving the law of nature. (1984, p. 669)

As a result, two goals can be identified for Jewish terrorism performed by this group: (a) "to make oppression so intolerable that insurrection was inevitable," and (b) "to frustrate every attempt to reconcile the respective parties" (Rapoport, 1984, p. 669). The Sicarii used effectively the dagger as a main weapon in their terrorist activities, and this group became known, sometimes, as the "dagger men" (Barghothi, 1996). The Sicarii did not last for a long period of time. However, their effect on the Jewish community was noticed later during the era of Menachem Begin, before the establishment of the state of Israel (Barghothi, 1996). The Sicarii appears to have become a role model for many modern Jewish terrorist groups.

Modern Jewish Terrorism

Modern Jewish terrorism started in the first half of the twentieth century in Palestine. Some Jewish groups used terrorism against the British forces until they achieved their independence. J. Barghothi (1996, p. 84) goes further and argues that the state of Israel was born out of terrorism against Britain and the people of Palestine, but now Israel is viewed as a legitimate sovereign state, despite the fact that its violence was widely condemned during its occurrence.

The Irgun Zvai Leumi, best known as the Irgun organization, was very active in Palestine before the establishment of the state of Israel. It consisted of hundreds of people who fought and used terrorism against the British and Arabs in Palestine. A famous representative of that organization is Menachem Begin, who later became the prime minister of Israel (Barghothi, 1996).

The establishment of the state of Israel did not stop terrorism in Palestine. Rather, this kind of violence continued between the Israelis and the Palestinians, and most terrorist acts in the Middle East pertain to conflict between these two parties. In the modern era, both Palestinians and Israelis have groups who use religion to justify their terrorist acts.

During the 1990s, remarkable terrorist attacks took place motivated by Judaism. On January 1, 1997, an off-duty Israeli soldier used his M-16 automatic machine gun against Arab shoppers in a crowded market in Hebron, claiming he was on a mission from God. This act was similar (in justification) to the 1994 attack on Arab worshippers at the Abrahimi Mosque, which for Jews represented The Cave of the Patriarchs, in Hebron by Dr. Baruch Goldstein, and the 1995 assassination of Prime Minister Yitzhak Rabin. All these acts, according to their perpetrators, were executed as religious missions in order to establish the "new religious kingdom on earth" (Juergensmeyer, 1997; Hanuer, 1995).

Also, some Jews used their religion to justify terrorism in the United States. The targets of Jewish extremism included individuals and organizations considered anti-Semitic or opposed to Israeli interests. The issue of Jewish terrorism in the United States, in general, focused on the activities of one organization, the Jewish Defense League (JDL). The JDL attacked "Soviet" targets (before the collapse of the Soviet Union), such as diplomatic installations, and personnel. In addition, the JDL listed and attacked Arab, Iranian, French, and German targets. Bombings were the primary means of attack followed by shooting, arson, vandalism, and kidnapping (Harris, 1987).

In 1968, Rabbi Meir Kahana founded the Jewish Defense League (JDL). The goal of this organization was to prevent attacks against Jewish people and their interests by Soviets, Arabs, and other anti-Jews. The JDL started its activities peacefully, but later indulged in violence and bombing attacks (George and Wilcox, 1992).

In 1971, Rabbi Meir Kahana moved from the United States to Israel and became a member of the Israeli parliament (Knesset). In 1985, the JDL was suspected of bombing the American-Arab Anti-Discrimination Committee headquarters in Boston. In the next several years, they attacked the Russian embassy in New York, the Russian embassy housing complex on Long Island, and were suspected of planting an explosive device in New York's J. F. Kennedy Center for the Performing Arts. They also attacked suspected Nazi war criminals (George and Wilcox, 1992; White, 1991; Mullins, 1997).

In 1990, Meir Kahana returned to New York, and after a speech at a Jewish function in New York City, he was assassinated by El Sayid al-Nosair (a Muslim), one of the terrorists convicted for the World Trade Center bombing (an act committed by Muslim terrorists). After Kahana's death the JDL became less active. However, with the death of Israel's Prime Minister Rabin, and the uncertainty of his death's effect on Middle East policies, the JDL's activities were expected to increase (Mullins, 1997).

CHRISTIANITY AND TERRORISM

Historical Terrorism

Unlike Judaism and Islam, early Christianity had no single messianic terror group occupying a prominent place. Also, Christian terrorism was not connected to underground organizations. Thus, Christian examples of early terrorism tended to be less secretive and better documented than those of Jewish and Islamic groups. For example, the crusades had a messianic but overt component which produced violence and about which much has been written. In the late medieval period the "Taborites" and the "Anabaptists" created some systems of state terror (Rapoport, 1988, p. 196).

Modern Christian Terrorism

Most right-wing terrorism in the United States has a religious (Christian) component. Many Christian organizations rely on their special interpretation of the Bible in committing violent (terrorist) acts. These include anti-Semitic attacks, anti-abortion acts, and violent anti-black movements.

For many right-wing extremists, the superiority of the white race is a basic belief. Therefore, blacks, other non-whites, and Jews are considered inferior racially, mentally, physically, and spiritually (Harris, 1987). The major Christian group of the right wing is the Christian Identity Movement (CIM). It has a religious belief that the whites, not the Jews, are the true descendants of Israel. Jews, to quote this movement, represent a "Satanic bloodline." Moreover, they believe the Bible is a history and guidebook of the non-Jewish white race that began with Adam (Harris, 1987).

Many of the far-right organizations have adopted the Christian Identity Movement philosophy. They believe that God's law must be re-established on the earth to set the stage for Jesus' return. Thus, the white race must reestablish dominance and control before the Second Coming of Christ can occur. To them, that means defeating the "agents of Satan" and the Jews, who are believed to control the world's governments as well as the United States. In addition, Christ will establish his Second Kingdom in the United States, so there is some religious justification for attacking the federal government (Holden, 1987). The far right organizations describe the federal government as the "Zionist Occupational Government (ZOG)" (Mullins, 1997).

To this type of Christian extremist, the argument is that violence against Jews and minorities is justified for several reasons: (1) Jews and minorities, according to extremist interpretations of the Bible, are not humans, and therefore killing them has no moral sanctions; (2) Jews are "agents of Satan," and it is very difficult to peacefully stop them from corrupting the world. Thus, violence is the only way to overthrow the ZOG; (3) These organizations in the right-wing literally interpret the New Testament book of Revelation and believe Armageddon is in the near future (White, 1986). When Armageddon happens, Christians will fight the "agents of Satan" and help speed the Second Coming of Christ.

In short, many of the far-right organizations reinterpret the Bible to suit their goals (Hoffman, 1997). For some militant religious groups, religion provides the grounds and the motivation for all their actions (Gallagher, 1997). Abortion clinic bombers also cite scripture to justify their acts. Other right-wing terrorist groups, including The Covenant, the Sword and the Arm of the Lord, and The Order, have used Scripture-based messianic perspectives for the same purpose (Rapoport, 1988). The group called the Aryan Nations follows a similar pattern. Most of these groups are from rural America, and over 80 percent are Protestant (Aho, 1990).

The Aryan Nations

The International Association of Chiefs of Police describes the Aryan Nations as "extremist, anti-Semitic, Neo-Nazis." Their belief is that Christ was not a Jew but an Aryan, white Anglo-Saxon, and that Jews are not the "chosen people," that the United States is the "Promised Land." Jews are viewed as "children of Satan" who must be exterminated (Stinson, 1987).

The Order

The Order was founded in 1983 as a splinter group of the Aryan Nations. Members felt that more extreme tactics (violent and terrorist) were required to achieve their goals. The Order considers all non-whites as "mud people," and enemies of the white race. Its members swear an oath to fight and eliminate their enemies. Each member of the group becomes an "Aryan Warrior" and must work toward accruing points based on the murder of Jews, blacks, federal judges, and FBI agents (Stinson, 1987).

In addition, two other groups in the right wing have similar beliefs and actions. These groups are (1) The Covenant, The Sword, and The Arm of The Lord, (2) Posse Comitatus or "power of the county" (Albanese, 1993). Also, the Ku Klux Klan (KKK), Defensive Action, anti-abortion groups, the Freemen Community in Montana, the Christian militia that supported Timothy McVeigh (the convicted bomber of the Oklahoma City federal building), and isolated groups such as the Branch Davidian in Waco can be placed under the category of far-right-wing terrorism. They share, to some extent, the same system of belief, based on religious foundations, in white control and power, and the perception of the immorality of government (Juergensmeyer, 1997; Kaplan, 1997).

In conclusion, the far-right-wing organizations consider themselves as being the protectors of the white race and their religion from their enemies. E. Gallagher (1997, p. 64) cited a quote of one of the right-wing extremists that best describes their mission; that is: "We are engaged in a struggle to the death between the people of the Kingdom of God and the Kingdom of Satan."

ISLAM AND TERRORISM

For most law enforcement agencies and researchers, "Islamic fanatics" are a source of domestic terrorism in the United States (Harris, 1987). The September 11, 2001, bombing of the World Trade Center (WTC) in New York has been the major terrorist act attributed to Islamic terrorism in the United States. This was after the 1993 bombing of the same buildings brought "the reality of Islamic terrorism in the United States, and it was the beginning of war between radical Islam and the U.S." (Bodansky, 1993, p. 396).

On the other hand, there are some experts on Islamic affairs who believe that to see Islam as a threat to the West and the US is just a misperception introduced by a small group of people. Some argue that the "Islamic threat" to the West and the US is an issue introduced by those who wanted new evils in the post-Cold War era (Esposito, 1995). For those, the WTC bombing created the fear of Islam, of radical Muslims who had bases in the US, and of a blind Egyptian cleric, Sheikh Omar Abd al-Rahman who was linked to these bases (p. 189).

In addition, Sheikh (Imam) Omar Abd al-Rahman is described as "the spiritual leader of the American Islamists community and the senior leader of the armed Islamist Movement in the United States" (Bodansky, 1993, p. 222–223). Most Americans see Islam as a threat in "terms of its extremists" (Karabell, 1995). Z. Karabell asked American college students in an elite university what they thought when the word "Muslim" is mentioned. Students' answers confirmed that they perceive Islam as a threat; some of these answers about Muslims were "gun-toting," "bearded," "fanatic terrorists hell bent on destroying the great enemy, the United States." In addition, Americans get most of their information from the media. Following the Oklahoma City bombing, many Americans heard experts on terrorism saying that the bombing was the "handy-work" of Middle East terrorists or Islamic fundamentalists (Esposito, 1995). That quick conclusion may have been due to the fact that the threat of Islamic terrorism is always present and that it has a long history.

Historical Islamic Terrorism

Many researchers and experts on terrorism trace the origin of Islamic terrorism to the eleventh century and connect it with the Assassins (e.g., Hoffman, 1997, 1995; Barghothi, 1996; Rapoport, 1988, 1984). The Assassins, known also as Ismailis-Nizari, survived for two centuries between 1090 and 1275 A.D. (Lewis, 1967). Their goal was to fulfill or purify Islam in a community where no separation between political and religious institutions existed (Rapoport, 1984).

The word "assassins" literally means "hashish eaters" in reference to the process of drugging young members to have the experience of living in Paradise. Paradise is the ultimate place in which martyrs live as a reward for their good deeds when they follow the doctrine of the Assassins, which focused on the concept of martyrdom (Barghothi, 1994). "Hashish eaters" (hashashin in Arabic) is a label used by Sunni Muslims to describe this group, although there is no evidence that drugs were used in their activities (Rapoport, 1984). Moreover, Assassins were terrorists which succeeded in building their own state, or a loose coalition of city-states, "to buttress their organization of terror" (Barghothi, 1996 p. 87). As a result, they carried out international terrorism which threatened a number of countries, specifically Persia and what is now Syria (Barghothi, 1996).

Although Assassins are described as terrorists and used real terrorist acts, there are no primary sources that allow us to know how they justified their tactics. What is well known about them is that they engaged in a struggle "to purify Islam and make extraordinary efforts to demonstrate that they act defensively" (Rapoport, 1984, p. 668). Finally, the Assassins originated from Islamic Shia and tried to persuade other Muslims to follow their faith (Lewis, 1967).

Modern Islamic Terrorism

Islam continues to be cited by Western media and literature as associated (more than other religions) with terrorism. The Islamic fundamentalists cause fear in Western countries (and some other parts of the world). They are considered as a specter which has inspired fear, and are, therefore, treated "with unusual degrees of prejudice" (Hyman, 1994, p. 234). Most of the recent focus on Muslims originated with the revolution in Iran, and the later collapse of the Soviet Union.

The Islamic revolution in Iran inspired many Islamic groups and organizations around the world. In Lebanon, for example, Hizbullah (Party of God, classified as a terrorist organization in the West) was established with the full support of Iran. Hizbullah (with a Shiite component) committed terrorist acts in Lebanon and elsewhere. Its members show a striking willingness to die for the sake of God, and are guaranteed a place in Paradise if they die while they are in Jihad (Rapoport, 1988). Jihad is most often translated as holy war.

Hoffman (1995: 274–275) cited three quotations from religious figures who are associated with Hizbullah and Iran (Shia):

> 1. "The world as it is today is how others shaped it" (Ayatollah Baqer al-Sadar), and he added "We have two choices: either to accept it (the shaped world) with submission, which means letting Islam die, or to destroy it, so that we can construct the world as Islam requires" (Mustafa Chamran).
> 2. "We are not fighting within the rules of the world as it exists today, we reject all those rules" (Mustafa Chamran).
> 3. Hussein Mussawai, the founder and leader of Hizbullah, who was assassinated in 1994 in an Israeli helicopter attack, remarked, "We are not fighting so that the enemy will recognize us and offer us something. We are fighting to wipe out the enemy."

Thus, Hizbullah began "launching human-bomb attacks against Israeli and other targets in Lebanon and other places which stunned the world with their new pattern of terrorism where both the perpetrator and the victims lose their lives" (Israeli, 1997).

Sunni Muslim organizations also performed terrorist acts. The Islamic Resistance Movement (best known as HAMAS) is another Islamic organization which has been listed in most countries, especially in the West, as one of the most dangerous terrorist organizations because of its suicidal acts in Israel. This organization is associated with the Sunni sect of Islam.

Hoffman cited the following statements of one of HAMAS's leaders: "Israel will exist and will continue to exist until Islam will obliterate it, just as it obliterated others before it." Sheikh (Imam) Ahmad Ibrahim, one of HAMAS's senior clerics, declared: "Six million descendants of monkeys (i.e., Jews) now rule in all the nations of the world, but their day, too, will come. Allah! Kill them all, do not leave even one" (1995, p. 275).

Until September of 2001, in the United States the 1993 bombing of the World Trade Center was the major terrorist act attributed to Islamic groups. The convicted bombers were a group of Muslim (Sunni), like-minded individuals, who worshipped at the same religious institution (Mosque) (Hoffman, 1997) and were associated with a religious figure (Sheikh and Imam Omar Abd al-Rahman). There was no evidence, until now, that this group was part of a terrorist organization within the United States.

Chapter 5

Research on Terrorism

Scientific literature and research on terrorism is hard to locate within the mass of journalistic accounts. Terrorism has been and is still seen by many as a political issue and a topic that only the federal government can deal with. Thus, in the United States, terrorism is an issue within the jurisdiction of the federal government which controls all aspects related to this topic.

Literature on "modern" religious-based terrorism begins with the early 1980s, because at this time the first modern international religious terrorism was identified (Hoffman, 1995). D. Rapoport (1984) described his article as "the first comparative study of religious terror groups." His article "Fear and Trembling: Terrorism in Three Religious Traditions" provides detailed analysis of doctrines and methods of three religious groups: the Thugs in Hinduism, the Assassins in Islam (Shia), and the Zealots-Sicarii in Judaism. The author utilized historical data to compare the three traditions, but did not deal with any human subjects and gathered no primary data.

Rapoport's study motivated others to study religion and terrorism, and most of the inquiry which followed relied heavily on his research. For example, B. Hoffman (1995), in his article "Holy Terror: The Implications of Terrorism Motivated by Religious Imperatives," explored the issue of religion and terrorism, but based it solely on a literature review. J. Barghothi (1996) followed with a comparison of historical terrorist organizations with modern ones based on analysis of archival data. He reviewed "some of the existing literature" about terrorist groups, and compared Sicarrii, Thugs, and Assassins (historical groups) with Narodnaya Volya (in Russia between 1878 and 1881), the Irgun Zvaileumi (in Israel), and the Algerian National Liberation Front (FLN) in Algeria (modern groups).

A. Schbley (1990) studied Lebanese Shi'a religious terrorists to identify some facts about the operational code of this group. He interviewed twenty-six Lebanese Shi'as who had been involved in the planning or execution of terrorist acts (ex-terrorists). His findings revealed that there is an operational code for this terrorist group. According to this code, American personnel and targets are the most attractive (pp. 238–239). These findings confirm the threat of this group to the United States. However, Schbley's study was done outside the United States with people who never lived in, or were involved with terrorist acts, in the United States. These subjects (in Schbley's study, the interviewees) were "family members" or "childhood friends" of the researcher. Schbley's study sheds some light on a major problem in doing research on terrorism, which is finding terrorists to participate in research projects on terrorism.

PROBLEMS OF RESEARCH ON TERRORISM

Research on terrorism presents special problems which make it difficult for researchers to conduct scientific research. Most of the information about terrorism comes from media sources and in some terrorist cases, from official records (Smith and Morgan, 1994). Thus, "there is very little research that empirically examines the motivations, psychological characteristics, or demographics of terrorists" (Mullins, 1997, p. 90). Generally, the available data for researchers concern specific terrorist incidents, and the most common sources for these data are newspapers reports and police records. Accurate and detailed case studies are usually classified and stored in government, military, and law enforcement agencies. As such, there are often considered intelligence data pertinent to national security and is not easily accessed (Yerushalmi, 1987).

Another problem in doing research on terrorism is the lack of clear and general definitions of the concept of terrorism, and the unclear relationship between terrorism and other concepts, such as political violence or warfare (Schmid, 1983). As T. Austin (1999) puts it, "it is difficult to arrive at a definition of terrorism which will please all scholars." A. Schmid (1987) collected 109 definitions of terrorism in the literature. M. Shukry (1991) argues that despite the thousands of published articles and books on terrorism, there is still no one acceptable or agreed upon definition of terrorism.

Besides, theories explaining terrorism are distributed over a wide range of different disciplines (Schmid, 1983), such as sociology, psychology, political science, and economics. Moreover, "entire articles have been devoted to the poor quality of terrorism research and the absence of a coherent theoretical model of terrorism" (Kissmane, 1989, p. 5). Finding one theory to explain the impact of terrorism on individuals is difficult, and perhaps it is most appropriate focus is to look to natural disaster research (Austin, 1996, 1991, 1989). The efforts that had been taken in the aftermath of major terrorist acts (i.e., World Trade Center attacks, and Oklahoma City bombing) are similar to those taken with earthquakes, floods, or other natural disasters. Indeed, FEMA (the Federal Emergency Management Agency) is getting more and more involved in terrorist attacks, although it has long been associated with natural disasters in the popular imagination.

Another problem facing researchers in the study of terrorism is the distinction between terrorism conducted by the state, and terrorism conducted by individuals and groups against the state (Barghothi, 1996). Most states give themselves the right to respond to terrorism in the name of self-defense, or protecting national interests. But, at the same time, a state labels and accuses individuals, groups, or even other states of being terrorists when they do violence against it (Daher, 1994).

In summary, most of the literature on terrorism focuses on international terrorism (Albanese, 1993), and this literature has very little to say about religious-based terrorism. Religious-based terrorism is an area that needs more research within both international and domestic arenas. As shown in this selective review, perceptions of religious leaders are neglected in the literature. An exhaustive review of the literature fails to uncover a single study emphasizing perceptions of religious leaders from Judaism, Christianity, and Islam to explore the issue of religion and terrorism.

One can make the argument that the research questions of this book are not fully answered in this literature review. The first research question, which addresses definitions of terrorism, remains a necessary focus. The literature confirms the problem of defining terrorism, and no satisfactory definition is provided in the literature on terrorism from a religious perspective. Thus, a need persists to search further for meaningful definitions of terrorism, particularly in regard to the link between religion and terrorism.

The second research question deals with justifications of religious-based terrorism. This issue also finds limited relevant literature, but clearly sets the stage for further inquiry. Neutralization theory, as first introduced in sociology and now heavily oriented in criminology, appears to provide a logical foundation for exploring how terrorists' acts may be rationalized, particularly from religious perspectives.

Regarding the third research question, which addresses policy matters, the scientific literature offers very little relevant information specific to religious-based terrorism. Most of the procedures in countering terrorism rely on the enhancement of penalties and enforcing new laws. The question remains how these statutes deter terrorists. For example, how does the death penalty (the most severe penalty in any law against terrorism) deter a person who is willing to sacrifice his/her life for a religious goal? There are some terrorists who are willing to go, without any hesitation, to their deaths, and they take with them lives of others. To deal with this kind of activity, policymakers must understand how and why these people go willingly to death. Religious leaders, the experts in their religion, may have some answers. Based on such in-depth inquiry, governments and decision makers can better understand and plan for this kind of violent behavior.

To complement the data of this book and to answer the three research questions, the researcher has interviewed a sample of religious leaders in a number of Northeastern states and asked them specific questions related to religious-based terrorism. In other words, the remaining parts of this book are based on data collected from respected figures in their religions to shed some light on the relationship between religion and terrorism.

Part II

Religious Leaders Speak

For this part of the book (Chapters 6–10), the author collected primary data from participants representing three major religions (Judaism, Christianity, and Islam) during the summer of 1998. The appendix explains the methodology of this research and contains detailed descriptions of how the researcher dealt with sampling and research design issues.

The following chapters include the responses to each of the general research questions of this book. Thus, the first section reports findings regarding the issue of defining terrorism from the subjects' perspective. This section is relatively brief because subjects did not spend much interview time explaining how they define terrorism and often responded with short definitions and in only a few sentences.

The next section in this part focuses on the second research question and presents findings on religious leaders' perceptions and attitudes toward justifying certain terrorist acts (i.e., when violence can, in fact, be justified from religious leaders' points of view). In this section, religious leaders were also asked to take the role of the other and to comment on how violence may be permitted from the offenders' perspective. In other words, in more of a role-play scenario, the participants took the role of terrorists as suggested by the researcher, and tried to speak on behalf of the terrorist in an effort to justify the use of violence. The responses were divided into three chapters organized by religion because participants provided considerable details on the issue concerning the justification of violence and terrorism in the name of religion.

The final section (Chapter 10) concerns the third research question which pertains to ideas and suggestions reported by the subjects on the issue of how to deal with terrorism in the name of religion (i.e., dealing with policy issues of how to counter this special kind of violence). It is rather a long section with participants expressing their opinions in a rather detailed account and with occasionally extended suggestions on how to discourage and control this kind of violence.

Chapter 6

Defining Terrorism

Each participant in the study was asked to define terrorism. There were significant differences between the participants concerning this issue. This disagreement goes in tandem with what has been introduced in the literature mentioned in Chapter 3. However, certain themes are observed in the participants' definitions. All the interviewees' definitions center around three main categories: the perpetrator, the victim or target, and the goal of the violent act. Each definition, to some extent, includes these themes; however, some differences are noticeable regarding certain issues within each theme.

PERPETRATOR

Although each definition has an element (theme) as reported by the participant, some definitions focus on individuals, groups and organizations, or states. Other definitions do not specify the perpetrator and, instead, focus on the act regardless of its performer. For example, one sheikh defines terrorism as "any violent act directed intentionally toward innocent civilians." This definition ignores the person responsible for the act and focuses on the victim or the target.

Thus, regardless of the perpetrator, as long as the violent act is directed against civilian targets, it will be considered terrorism from this participant's perspective. Similarly, one priest, for example, does not focus on the perpetrator and define terrorism as "any act of violence or threat of violence that denies basic human dignity and respect to any individual." These definitions are rather vague and do not mention anything about the terrorist perpetrator. A Jewish perspective is very similar to the other two perspectives in dealing with the actor element in defining terrorism. However, the focus is on group-related activity in using violence. A rabbi defines terrorism as "the use of violence against a population for the purpose of affecting their political leaders."

Most of the definitions from Jewish and Christian subjects focus on individuals and groups or organizations when they mention the perpetrator element of defining terrorism. None of these subjects mentions the state, as an actor, in the definition of terrorism. For example, one rabbi states that "an individual, an organized group, or any political entity" can carry out terrorism.

A priest also includes individuals and groups in his definition when he defines terrorism as "an unjust act of violence . . . by either an individual or group designed to force the people who are being terrorized to do what the terrorists want them to do."

To the contrary, some of the Muslim subjects do consider the state as a potential perpetrator of terrorism. For example, one Sunni Imam remarked that the state of Israel kills innocent Arab and Muslim people of the West Bank and Lebanon. He consider such actions terrorism. The Imam drew an analogy between Israeli soldiers and suicide bombers as both killing innocent people; yet the Imam remarked, killing done by one side only (suicide bombers) is labeled as terrorism by Western media. The Imam said, "The Israeli Army kills innocent women and children, and the suicide bombers kill civilians too. But how can this army have the right to do so, while the Palestinians have no right to defend themselves and are accused of being terrorists?" A Shiite Imam described the Israeli attacks against South Lebanon as terrorism perpetrated by a state. "Israel used violence against innocent people in Lebanon and killed many civilians and non-military targets. Yet nobody in the West considers this terrorism."

Paradoxically, one rabbi chose not to describe what was going on in South Lebanon, between the Israelis and the Lebanese Hizbullah, as terrorism. In his definition, he excludes this kind of armed conflict in Lebanon as terrorism. Neither of the two sides (Israel and Hizbullah) are committing terrorist acts, according to his definition. This rabbi comments that, "It is very difficult to say there is terrorism going on in Southern Lebanon, because there are Israeli soldiers with the soldiers of the Southern Lebanese Army" (an army allied with the Israelis). The rabbi describes the situation there as "a stated hostility between Hizbullah and armed forces in South Lebanon. They (both sides) know that they are going to attack each other. So, for me this is not terrorism."

TARGETS

Conceptualizing the target, as a factor, is the second main theme of defining terrorism. All definitions, given by the subjects of this study, consider attacking innocent civilian targets as the major factor in defining terrorism. For them, attacking innocent civilian people is the tool by which an act can be classified as terrorism.

Some of the Jewish subjects, however, consider attacks against military targets as terrorism and report such in their definitions. For those Jewish respondents, attacking military targets in non-war times is considered terrorism. Many Muslim participants, on the other hand, take the opposite position. They recognize and approve attacking military targets of an enemy at any time, and they do not consider such acts as terrorism.

In short, the issue of whether targets represent civilians and innocent people is the number one reason to classify a violent act as terrorism. The following quotes from different subjects illustrate this finding. A Muslim Imam stated that "any violent act directed intentionally toward innocent civilians represents terrorism." A rabbi similarly responded, "Attacking primarily civilian targets, or civilians themselves for the purpose specifically of causing civilian damage or casualties, whether or not it is a time of war, represents terrorism." The rabbi continued, "Or even a military target, if it is a time without a clear declaration of war or open warfare would represent terrorism."

A Christian religious leader suggested, "An attack on civilians, innocent people, for the purpose of attaining some larger goal represents terrorism." A Catholic priest extended the definition of terrorism based on the target element to include other types of traditional crimes, for example domestic violence. For this participant, violence against women is also terrorism based on religion. In his words, "certain Biblical passages (e.g., Numbers 5:22, Isaiah 3:17–18) sanction inter-personal terrorism; that is, violence against women." Other types of terrorism include "gang violence, drive by shooting, and domestic abuse against the elderly."

Hence, using targets or victims to define terrorism expands the scope of terrorism. One can include in his/her definition of terrorism any type of violent act.

GOALS OF VIOLENCE

The goal of a violent act against a specific target is of major importance in the process of defining terrorism. All participants in this study agree that terrorists strive for nonpersonal goals. The subjects include in their definitions political, religious, and/or social objectives as goals of terrorism. Each subject points to the goal of terrorism to be a logical reference point from the actor's perspective. Some terrorists fight for achieving political objectives such as independence or liberation of certain territories. Others fight to "please God" and for specific divine ends, as mentioned in a Holy Scripture. The final goals for other terrorists might be social ends such as fighting unjust policies in society.

One rabbi argues in his definition that the goal of terrorism is "either the removal of some political opponent, or to retaliate for some injustice, or to prevent what is believed to be some injustice . . . terrorism is always connected with political things, there is never a case of terrorism only because God wants us to do violence for a religious goal." In a similar fashion, another rabbi defines terrorism as "unauthorized, unjustified attack and murder of noncombatants for the sake of a political goal."

On the other hand, a priest claims in his definition that the goal could be anything. Thus, the goal of terrorism is to force the people who are being terrorized to do anything the terrorists want them to do. Another priest considers terrorism (i.e., in Ireland) as being a "just political struggle between two sides." A Muslim participant also focuses on the political ends of terrorism. He points to the fact that "most of what is called Islamic terrorism is directed to liberate Palestine and South Lebanon from the Israeli occupation;" that is, "we want our complete rights in our complete land." Regarding the goal of religious-based terrorism, all participants mention that implementing the "true religion" (or their interpretation of religion in society) is the ultimate goal of this kind of terrorism.

Without question, definition is a most problematic issue in dealing with this kind of violence. It is difficult to reach an agreed-upon definition of religious terrorism. One priest, for example, answers the question regarding definition by saying:

I do not know how to define terrorism; there are always two sides of a story. What makes it a terrorist act I do not know. I do think when news reports show young children suffering terribly, dying as a result, you know, of a bomb in a market place somewhere... then I get a reaction. I say that is wrong. But then I am not on the other side. You know! I do not know the kind of pain and suffering, I do not know the kind of conditions that lead a person to commit an act like that. I could see that the person I am calling the terrorist might look at me and say you are no less a terrorist than I am.

A rabbi also points to the difficulty in defining terrorism from a purely Jewish perspective. He further notes that "the word terrorism does not appear in Jewish traditional writings. There is no Hebrew word for terrorism."

As mentioned, regardless of the differences and disagreements about defining terrorism, most subjects in the three groups agree that terrorism is a violent act against innocent civilian targets by individuals or groups to achieve certain goals. It is difficult to reach a definition of religious-based terrorism. Some of the participants claim that there is a bias against their religion when people define terrorism. For example, one Imam argues that, "the media has never classified non-Muslim individuals, who commit violence, with their religion. For example, you never hear of 'Christian terrorists.' The abortion clinic bombing, where nurses and doctors are killed, is not called [Christian] religious terrorism. This is [so] in spite of the fact that these acts are perpetrated by religious fanatics." Another example, according to the Imam, is when Dr. Baruch Goldstein entered Al-Ibrahimi Mosque in Hebron, in the fasting month of Ramadan, and killed more than fifty worshipers in the Mosque. He was not classified as a Jewish terrorist. In fact, he was a hero in the eyes of some of the Jewish community. "His grave became a place of Jewish pilgrimage." On the other hand, the Imam adds, when a Muslim is involved (in a violent act) it becomes news and he is classified as a Muslim terrorist. "There is a bias against Muslims." This bias of one religious perspective against another appears to overshadow the issue of defining religious-based terrorism from an Islamic perspective.

A Christian participant also states that religious-based terrorism is beyond the scope of Christianity. He adds, "I guess this is one of those places where Christians are probably talking with forked tongues, out of both sides of their mouth at one time, because I do not think the Christian religion could advocate the use of violence or terrorism."

As a result, among the participants from the three religions in this study, there is a tendency to not recognize any violence as terrorism in the name of their own religion when it comes to defining religious-based terrorism. Most subjects from each religion try to exclude their religion from this kind of violence and refuse to accept the idea that there is terrorism in their religion.

Hence, defining religious-based terrorism in this study has proven to be an arduous task.

Still, this disagreement on defining terrorism is also clearly evident in the literature. As pointed out in Chapter 3, A. Schmid (1983) collected 109 definitions of terrorism in general. There is no reliable source on the number of definitions of religious-based terrorism, but one can make the argument that we expect to have many definitions for this kind of violence based on what Schmid has found regarding traditional terrorism.

Disagreement on defining terrorism among the subjects, and the denial of the existence of terrorism within a religion in certain cases, lead us to the issue of justifying religious-based terrorism. Following from the varied definitions and sometimes suggestions of bias, all of the subjects reject any kind of justification for terrorist acts in the name of their religion. To the contrary, all of them condemn terrorism according to their specific definitions. However, many of the subjects provide their perceptions and attitudes toward justifying the use of force and violence. Violence in these cases is not considered terrorism and it is permitted according to their religion. The next section explains cases in which the use of violence might be justified.

JUSTIFICATION OF VIOLENCE/TERRORISM

Chapters (7-9) are organized to present the findings regarding the second research question (i.e., what are the perceptions and the attitudes of religious leaders regarding the justification of certain terrorist acts?) by the major religious schools of thought. Participants were asked about their own perceptions and attitudes in justifying terrorism, and how they feel the terrorists themselves might justify their terrorist violence.

As mentioned, all religious leaders give justifications for some violence in certain cases. But, according to their definitions of terrorism, all religious leaders agree on the difficulty of actually justifying terrorism, that is, religious leaders deny any kind of justification for terrorism, as they define it. Yet, when asked how offenders might justify religious-based violence, the participants, clearly, provide some justification for certain terrorist acts. Nevertheless, for many of the religious leaders, this justification is not acceptable within their mainstream religion. In short, religious leaders' perceptions and attitudes are against any justification of terrorism. However, when the leaders do justify some violent acts, they do not label these acts as terrorism but as justified violent acts.

Justifying terrorism in the name of religion is very difficult from the perspective of the subjects. None of them claimed that religion might justify terrorism. Instead, each participant argues that his religion is against terrorism as it is defined. However, many respondents say that their religion might justify certain violent acts under special circumstances, such as fighting a "just war," acting in "self-defense," "protecting others' lives," "resisting an oppression of an occupation" or a "corrupted government," or "preventing future violence." Despite these limited justifications, no respondent believes that violence is warranted against innocent or civilian targets.

Data regarding justifications for terrorism are divided into two categories. First, how do religious leaders themselves perceive this violence and is it a justifiable act? Second, how might terrorists (themselves) justify their violence in the name of religion (i.e., when religious leaders try to speak on behalf of those terrorists)? In the first category, participants were asked to express their perceptions and attitudes toward the justifications of terrorism in the name of God. The questions were focused on their own ideas and how this kind of violence could or should be justified. In the second category, participants were asked to try to speak in the language, or the terminology, of the perpetrators of religious-based terrorism (i.e., a kind of role-playing).

To render the data and the responses regarding these justifications more understandable and interesting, participants were asked to give examples of what they consider as terrorist acts occasionally attributed to religiously motivated perpetrators. Then the subjects were asked how these acts might be justified from a religious point of view. In certain cases, when a participant did not give an example, the interviewer would do so. The interviewees and the interviewer gave highly publicized terrorist acts as examples of religious-based terrorism. These acts include, but are not limited to, the assassination of Yitzhak Rabin; the massacre of Hebron (by Jewish individuals); suicide bombers incidents in the Middle East; the 1993 bombing of the World Trade Center in New York City (by Muslim perpetrators); the conflict in Ireland; and anti-abortion bombings (by Christian protesters).

Many of the Jewish and Muslim respondents, however, focused their accounts on the Arab-Israeli conflict and gave detailed justifications related to this struggle. Because of this conflict, Jewish participants gave the longest responses. They were more open compared to the other two categories. Christian subjects, on the other hand, generally gave the shortest answers and did not spend as much time on this conflict, but talked instead about the conflict in Ireland and other places in Europe. The length of the responses is an interesting area for further research to understand why Jewish participants gave the longest answers. The next sections introduce data regarding the justifications of religious-based terrorism, starting with those of religious leaders. The data are organized according to the participant's responses. Nevertheless, Muslim responses were combined to include both the religious leaders' perspective and the actors' perspective; there was no significant difference between the two perspectives, whereas a clear difference was noted in the other two religions between the two perspectives.

Thus, the first two sections (Jewish and Christian justifications) consists of the two perspectives (their own responses and their role-playing ones). This division is necessary due to the length of these responses, and to the varied justifications associated with each religion.

Chapter 7

Jewish Justifications

Jewish law does not present any justification for terrorism, but the use of violence may be justified in certain cases. The religious leaders who participated in this study do not accept any terrorism in the name of their religion. They all agree that it is very rare to find a true justification in their religion for this kind of violence, especially when civilian targets are involved.

One rabbi, who was ordained thirty years ago, mentions that Judaism never justified terrorism and said, "I do not think that within Judaism one can make an argument that terrorism is a morally acceptable act."

Another rabbi, also ordained almost two decades ago, adds, "There is no such religious-based terrorism (in Judaism) and no one can claim the role of prophets to speak of terrorism in the name of God."

A third rabbi, with a long experience (more than forty years as a rabbi), argues that:

Jews do not have the history of aggression and violence against non-Jews from a religious perspective in a wholesale fashion . . . We do not believe in wholesale murder, we do not believe in wholesale violence. Generally with the Jewish tradition, terrorism is always connected with political things . . . There is never a case of terrorism because God wants us to do violence for a religious goal. An important point to consider here in studying Jewish violence (terrorism) is that none of it has had the approval of a prominent religious leader ever . . . I have heard no case where any respected religious leader or chief rabbi came out in favor of a terrorist act (done by a Jew).

The disapproval of terrorism in the name of religion in Judaism goes from the general to the specific (i.e., to certain terrorist acts). All Jewish subjects express their disapproval of the attack against Muslims in Hebron. They consider that incident as a terrorist one. Many of them say it is an unjustifiable act from a religious perspective. For example, one rabbi, who has been to Israel many times and is well informed about the situation there, classifies the act of

Israeli's killing Muslim worshipers in the Ibrahimi Mosque in Hebron as a "massacre," and as a terrorist act. He says, "The act has to be condemned. I dare say if Abraham had been asked at that moment, should I shoot people in the back, the answer would be no."

No Jewish subject approves of, or believes a justification was possible for the assassination of Yitzhak Rabin (the prime minister of Israel who was killed in 1995), because non-violent means were available to show disagreement with Rabin. As one rabbi says, "If you disagree with the man (Rabin) vote him out of the office." Thus, one should use political and peaceful means to get rid of a political leader, not violence.

Despite this total rejection of terrorism or using violence in the name of Judaism, Jewish respondents acknowledge the fact that their religion may justify the use of violence in specific situations such as self-defense or the case of just war. Yet even in these cases, using violence should be the last resort, the rabbis emphasize. In other words, if violence can be avoided and nonviolent means are available, then violence is not justified. The first and the foremost situation, in which violence may be justified, is the case of saving lives. As one rabbi puts it, "the major religious sanction representing a permission for violence is the need to save life."

Another rabbi explained the permission of killing as this:

If I am going to deprive you of your life you will have to have committed a capital crime, or we have to be officially at war. To me, as a Reform rabbi, the idea of upholding God's Law by killing God's children is aptly absurd. I have to be really oppressed to take another human being's life... It has to be for survival.

In Judaism, it has been noted, one may also justify violence for self-defense. As a rabbi explains, "One has the right to use violence in order to protect another person or persons, and therefore violence in this instance protects the Jewish people . . . Violence is permissible within Judaism, first and foremost for self defense."

Although Jewish rabbis condemn the assassination of Yitzhak Rabin, and describe it as a terrorist act, one Orthodox rabbi, who was ordained more than thirty years ago, does not consider that act as a terrorist one. He deplores the act of killing Rabin, but he says that this act might be justified under Jewish law as saving others' lives. Justification, the rabbi elaborates, might be as follows:

I do not see it (the assassination) as a terrorist act . . . It seems to be that the argument that has been made for the assassination of Rabin is one that is rooted in Jewish law. I think it is a misinterpretation of the Jewish Law, but it is rooted in Jewish law. In Jewish law, if someone is pursuing you, you have the right to kill that person in order to save your life. If someone is pursuing another individual in order to kill him and you are an innocent bystander, you have a right to take the pursuer's life. Now the argument that was made is that by negotiating with Palestinians, Jewish citizens of Israel were put in mortal danger, because Jews living in lands that would be ceded to the Palestinians would have no protection. And therefore, Rabin, who was doing the negotiating, was in fact one who has the same status as a pursuer. And, therefore, as an innocent bystander you have the right to protect these people who are being pursued by killing Rabin . . . Some rabbis declared Rabin a pursuer who needed to be killed before he caused other deaths.

In addition, the same rabbi insists that the land of Israel is holy and some rabbis may justify violence to maintain this land. Thus, in a time of war, violence may be justified, but not against civilians. Even during wartime, Judaism does not justify all kinds of violence. Violent acts against people who are not fighting are not justified, and there are certain rules which should be followed during war. The rabbi adds the following:

I think there is probably a pretty sizable, certainly not a majority, but a much larger minority of Orthodox rabbis who would argue that violence to maintain the land (of Israel) is permissible. So, the predominant position taken by the Orthodox community in Israel is one which says that Jewish law does not permit giving that land away, with some exceptions, the general principle is that this is part of the Biblical Land of Israel, and therefore, it cannot be given away.

To conclude, non-Orthodox rabbis do not give any religious justifications for the assassination of Yitzhak Rabin, nor for the attack against Muslims in Hebron, when they express their attitudes and perceptions. However, some Orthodox rabbis, although they do not approve of the act, seem to acknowledge certain religious justifications for the killing of Yitzhak Rabin, but they do not label this act as a terrorist one. For them, the pursuer argument justifies the killing according to Jewish law. Regarding the attack against Muslims, some Orthodox rabbis may give religious justifications for that act, under the pretext that Jewish lives are being protected or that the aim is to protect Jewish lives. Additional details on this specific issue are provided in the next section, justifications from the perpetrators' perspectives.

Jewish respondents were asked to speak on behalf of those perpetrators of violent acts in the name of their religions. More specifically, the question was, "If you were in the place of those who used violence in the name of religion, how might those terrorists justify their violent acts?" Jewish respondents gave many religious justifications for certain terrorist acts when they, as rabbis, spoke from the offender's perspective. The rabbis were asked how they, as rabbis, believe that terrorists might justify, in the name of religion, for example, the assassination of Yitzhak Rabin and the attack against Muslims in Hebron.

One Reform rabbi, with more than fifty years in service and a strong academic background in both religion and history, summarized the process of justification from the perpetrator's side as follows: "They (terrorists) think that they have the truth and the absolute truth. Anything else that is contrary to it is evil, is bad, and it should be eradicated."

Justifications from the Jewish terrorists' perspectives revolve around certain themes which overlap, to some extent, with what was mentioned in justifications from the religious leaders' perspectives.

IMPLEMENTING RELIGIOUS LAWS

A Conservative rabbi, with a long period of service, argues that some Jews might think that by resorting to violence for religious goals, they are implementing religious laws. For them, the rabbi comments, "Judaism teaches that Jerusalem is the capital of the Jewish people, and that it is a violation of Jewish law to permit non-Jews to rule the city of Jerusalem." Although the rabbi himself disagrees with using violence to maintain Jewish authority over Jerusalem, he says that few people would use violence "to bring about that purpose."

Another Reform rabbi points to a small group within Judaism (mainly Orthodox) who believe that for Jewish religious goals, they should get rid of the Arabs and their mosque, the Alaqsa Mosque, in Jerusalem. The rabbi describes this group as follows:

There is a group of people, Jews, who want to get the Temple Mount in Jerusalem back under Jewish hands (according to Jewish law). So, they would like to get rid of the Mosque (Alaqsa Mosque in Jerusalem). This is a small group to begin with, but in the group, there are a few who think violence is appropriate to do so. Violence may help physically to get rid of the mosque and would encourage conflict to either fight the Arabs away, or to, somehow, gain Jewish control of the Temple Mount. Keep in mind, for religious Jews; the land of Israel is holy ground.

SELF-DEFENSE AND/OR TO PROTECT THE LIVES OF OTHERS

Not only in Jewish responses, but also in Islam and Christianity as well, self-defense is the single most cited reason to justify violence, from both the perspectives of religious leaders and the actors. All respondents from the three religions justify the use of violence for self-defense and protecting the lives of others. As one rabbi puts it, the use of "violence is permissible within Judaism first and foremost for self-defense."

The second major factor in justifying violence (and terrorism), and also a factor associated with self-defense, is to stop the killing of other people. As for protecting others' lives, an Orthodox rabbi, who was ordained in 1978, traveled to Israel many times and actually lived there for two years, argues that "some people may justify the assassination of Yitzhak Rabin as being an act of killing a murderer, which is permissible according to Jewish law." From the perspective of an actor of this type of violence, the rabbi gives the following justification for the assassination of Yitzhak Rabin:

The assassination of Yitzhak Rabin might be justified as a killing of a murderer. Rabin was going to make peace with the Arab countries, even at the expense of Israel's security, so he was perceived as a murderer. According to Jewish Law, a murderer must be killed if that killing will stop a murder. So, according to this law, if you see a person about to murder another person, and absolutely the only way you can stop the murder is to kill that person, then you are allowed, . . . required not just permitted, to kill the assassin.

In other words, if you were standing and you see someone taking aim and about to fire on another individual, you are required to kill him (the killer), if the only way to stop it (the murder) is to kill him.

Another Orthodox rabbi, with almost the same long experience, agrees that the right to kill the killer is supported by Jewish law. The respondent maintains that Rabin was perceived as "a murderer and a traitor," two crimes punishable by death according to Jewish law. He adds, from an actor's perspective, the actor "felt religiously that after 2,000 years of exile and finally returning to Israel, that we were being sold out. We, the Jewish people, were being sold out by a traitor and that the death of the traitor is the penalty for treason."

In contrast to these justifications from an Orthodox perspective of killing Yitzhak Rabin, are those of a Reformed rabbi who has also been to Israel many times and who has worked as a rabbi for the last thirty years. He argues:

No one can make a blanket statement of Jewish opinion because Jewish theologians have debated many issues. However, there are some people who believe in the appropriateness of justifying the killing of Jews by other Jews. The major religious sanction or permission for violence...is the need to save life. For some religious extremists, it is clear that Rabin is taking the people down to destruction, and he must be stopped to save the nation. Therefore, it is proper to get rid of him by any possible means, and if the only means is assassination, then that should be done.

The rabbi respondent continues:

If the prime minister of Israel would be a traitor to his country and was deliberately trying to destroy the nation and leave it open and defenseless, to be conquered by its enemy, that person will be the cause of deaths of many thousands of innocent people.

The rabbi maintains that in the classic case of Jewish law, if someone is trying to shoot someone else, you are obligated to do anything you can to save the victim. If the only way to save the victim is by shooting the murderer, you can consider that a good deed. If you now, pushing that to a political realm, had a traitor who was deliberately trying to cause the death of innocent people, then you would be religiously encouraged to kill him.

"Bad People" and the "Land of Israel"

Regarding justifications of terrorism and violent acts by Jews against non-Jews, an Orthodox rabbi ordained ten years earlier gives two reasons. "Non-Jews are considered as 'no good' people living in the land of Israel; and, for the sake of the security of the state of Israel, (they) may have to be killed." The rabbi explains the first point as follows:

Some Jews have developed an attitude that advocates (that) non-Jews are no good based on some statements in the Bible or the Talmud that speak about non-Jews as pagans.

Unfortunately, some Jews may reflect this ethnocentrism that, somehow, shows that everybody else is bad. For those Jews "God said conquer the Land (of Israel) and throw out the nations, and not to make any deal with them ... because those nations are evil, rotten, pagen murders."

The rabbi goes on to say "pagans are described as people with no morals, no sense of justice, no sense of God. Pagans were seven nations which lived in Canaan. The Bible says of the nations living in Israel . . . 'when you conquer the Land, you shall kill them all and make no deals with them'."

Although the rabbi himself does not agree with this theological reasoning, and assures that the seven nations are limited to those ancient times, he says that some Jews might "take that out of context and say, oh good, there are Arabs living in Israel. We should kill them all, and make no deals with them."

The rabbi continues by stating, "Some other Jews might say God has given us the Land back after 3,000 years. We are required to do everything to maintain it. There is no Jewish life without the homeland." The rabbi's account clearly argues that violence against non-Jews can be justified in order to protect the land of Israel. Furthermore, another rabbi who was ordained more than fifty years ago gives a corroborating report:

For religious people it is difficult to give up the Land, because in every prayer, in grace at the meal, and in the prayer of going to bed, and the wedding party, everywhere they have prayed for the return to Jerusalem. They never gave up the claim of the Land. Arabs do not accept the existence of the Jews; they want to drive the Jews out of the Land, and that is the reason of the violence and war between the two sides there. Jews only defended themselves. They want to protect themselves on the Land. So it was forced upon them (Jews) to fight, and they do not do any violence, only defend themselves.

Another possibility of justifying violence against non-Jews pertains to the issue of sustaining the security of Israel once the state has been officially established. The issue here is not to necessarily go against any non-Jew, but to defend the state against attack. An Orthodox rabbi explains that "the consequence of a breach in security is potentially severe and has repeatedly caused Jewish life to be lost . . . so that breaching the security of Israel might motivate some Jews to respond and protect the state by doing violent acts." Thus, the argument is:

We are not required to lie down and die if we are attacked; we are going to defend ourselves. The Arab World pushed us into that situation, because nobody ever said let us destroy the Arabs. But, in the Arab World there are repeated calls for death and destruction of Jews and of Israel, and to push them (the Jews) into the sea. We do not say things like that.

The rabbi continued with more elaboration:

There have been cases where in Israel and the territories of the West Bank, some (Jewish) settlers responded to Arab violence by their own violence; for instance, the attack against Muslims in the Mosque of Hebron by a Jewish person. The actor of that attack,

Goldstein, who shot the worshipers in the Mosque . . . it is likely he was motivated by what he felt was an attempt to prevent violence against the Jewish community. Those who defended him say that there is evidence that there was going to be an attack on the Jews by the local Arabs, and he went and killed these worshipers in the hope of preventing this attack. Some say he sacrificed his own life, knowing he would die, in order to save the Jewish community, and that was proper.

JUST WAR

The idea of the just war is another justification which emerges from several reports of rabbi respondents based on their own attitudes and the actor's perspective or taking the role of the terrorist. The idea of a just war can invoke a rationale for using violence, and several rabbi subjects agree with this kind of justification when it is used in a traditional war, such as when one army fights another army.

One rabbi states, "Judaism does permit a just war." So, those who justify Goldstein's act (i.e., attacking Muslims in the mosque), argue that he felt "the Arabs were at war with the Jews, and then to prevent an attack or wipe out the enemy you kill some innocent people." They [those rabbis who accept this argument] felt that "such violence was permitted under the laws of war. A war for defense or to maintain security."

A rabbi who visited Israel many times says that he read and listened to the following logic from other Jews for justifying violence against non-Jews in Israel. He explains this rationale as follows:

The Arabs all around us in Israel want to kill us. They want to get rid of us. We are at war whether it is official or not, and as they (the Arabs) do not commit violence, there is no reason to hurt them. When they attack us, if we do not respond, that is just going to encourage more violence. The only way to stop violence is to respond so swiftly and powerfully that they will decide it is not worth it. So, they shoot at us, we will shoot at them. One of us wounded, two of them will be killed. Doing that is not for punishing them [the Arabs], but the purpose is stopping further violence. If you do not do it, respond in kind, it is not going to stop; it is the only way to bring peace.

Chapter 8

Christian Justifications

Christian religious leaders do not accept any justification of terrorism in the name of their religion. Many of them consider that any terrorist act for religious goals is not, and could not be, justified. However, the Christian religious leaders, as in the case of the Jewish leaders, recognize the possibility of justifying the use of violence (not terrorism) in their religion based on some religious principles. Moreover, they give some justifications for certain terrorists' acts when they take the role of others (the role of terrorists).

NO JUSTIFICATION

The ideal situation in Christianity, according to all Christian participants of the study, is that the use of violence cannot be justified, and they stressed the pacifist nature of Christianity. One Catholic priest, who has served in a church for the last fifteen years and teaches in a religious institution, explains:

The ideal in Christianity is always non-violence, is always pacifist. The command of Jesus to "love thy neighbor" is paramount. Yet, The Orthodox Church has generally accepted the possibility of violence, some violent acts, being just and right.

A Protestant priest describes any exploitation of Christianity to justify terrorism as invalid and labels such attempts as "a crock." He does not accept the Ku Klux Klan (KKK) claim that members act for the sake of Christianity. The priest refers to KKK violence as having no relation to Christianity. According to him:

A classic example of terrorism in this country is the KKK. Historically, the vast majority of these individuals were good, law-abiding, God-fearing, and churchgoers and they were often the upstanding pillars of their church community. But, when they swore what they are doing now is saving and protecting Christianity from the evil, that is a crock. Their real concern was to protect white society from people who they considered to be inferior.

Therefore, the priest continues, any claim to justify terrorism in the name of Christianity is not accepted because Jesus did not teach to kill other people as the terrorists do. Similarly, a Catholic priest remarks:

Jesus never taught us to go out and rape and pillage, to go out and kill people; he taught a very different way of life . . . The church teaches that there are eight deadly sins, and one of them is hate. Terrorism is bound up very much in hate. There is literally no place for hate in the faith . . . The KKK based their activities on hate, and any kind of Christian sugar coating on their activities is just an excuse, a way of allowing themselves to feel good about hanging a black man or burning a cross on a Catholic lawn, or whatever they had to do.

Another priest, with more than twenty years of service in churches, rejects any possibility of justifications for terrorism. He states, "The church can never condone a terrorist act; there is no justification for that kind of act because terrorism normally is premeditated violence."

Although Christianity does not advocate any terrorist acts, many of the participants point out the possibility of justifying violence in certain situations.

The following principles are derived from the religious leaders' responses and can be seen as religious-based justifications: self-defense; just war; and double-effect principles. The following sections explain these principles from the religious leaders' perspectives. As mentioned, self-defense and just war are the most repeated themes among all participants regardless of the position they take in justifying violence or terrorism.

SELF-DEFENSE

Violence in Christianity may be justified in a self-defense situation. All Christian respondents agree that individuals may use violence (not terrorism) to defend their lives, but this use of violence should be the last resort. If there is any way to avoid violence, then people must use it.

An Eastern Orthodox priest, with many years of service, justifies violence for individuals to protect their lives with the following statement:

The individual has the right to personal integrity and may defend oneself against an unjust attack. The individual may perhaps, even more, have the duty to protect a third party, an innocent third party from an unjust attack, even if such defense would require killing the attacker.

Not only are individuals permitted to use violence, but also the state can use violence to protect the lives of its citizens. The same priest further explains:

The church does recognize that it is possible that the state may, for instance, kill an individual in order to protect society. The state may defend its country from unjust aggression in order to protect its citizens, because that is its job.

Violence can, in some situations, then, be acceptable and justified by Christianity.

JUST WAR

Also in Christianity, the just war rationale is another principle by which violence is permitted. In the case of such a war, violence may be justified since the goal of just war must be a good goal. However, most wars can not be classified as just. Certain conditions must be met before accepting a war as just. A Protestant priest explains, "Just war violence may be justified for a future good of society." This justification is based on the following argument:

The closest we ever come to allow for the use of violence would be just warfare... but in just war three conditions must be met. The war must be on the authority of the sovereign (i.e., the king or the government); the cause has to be just and for the advancement of good, and/or the avoidance of evil. Saint Thomas Aquinas proposed these conditions in the fourteenth century. Augustine, also, defended the idea of just war, but it has to be undertaken for the good of society, it is defensible, and the end of war is peace.

Another priest points to the fact that many Christians consider the Crusades as a just war to defend the Holy Land; however, he disagrees with that assumption. "The Christian Crusaders in the Middle Ages were theoretically fighting to defend Jerusalem and the Holy Land from the evil Muslim terrorists. But the results show that was not the point or the purpose of that war." Despite the approval of the principle of just war, many priests admit that it is very difficult to meet the conditions of this kind of war. Most of the current wars are not just wars, according to the Christian belief.

DOUBLE EFFECT

Another distinctive justification for violence according to Christianity is the principle of double effect, that is, choosing one bad choice, if you have two or more bad choices, for a good end. This principle is explained by a Catholic priest who has more than twenty years of religious experience. According to the priest, one can justify violence by choosing an alternative (itself bad) for a good result, as in the case of the bombardment of Japan in World War II. He adds:

In Catholicism, there is something called the principle of "double effect." That is, if we are faced with a choice and both of these choices result in a bad outcome, and one of them has to be chosen, then you choose the choice that brings about the greater good. A good example of that would be during World War II when the bombs were dropped at Hiroshima and Nagasaki. It is an evil choice to make, taking the lives of all those people, but you look at the outcome. It would bring the end of the war, which would ultimately save billions of lives in all of Europe or destroy this group of people here. They are both wrong; they both have destructive outcomes, but which of these outcomes brings about the greatest good for humanity? We are always forced to make choices; you can use that principle with any situation in life.

Despite the possibility of using the above principle, the priest emphasizes that terrorism can not be justified. He argues, "Terrorism is not a justifiable act. And this is consistent with the Catholic view. And I do not think that bad means justify an end in terrorism."

Christian religious leaders give justifications for the use of violence (not terrorism) in specific situations. However, these leaders identify the reasons for some Christian terrorist acts as, due either to a misreading of the Bible, or their belief that such violent acts are pro-life demonstrations (as in the case of abortion). Nevertheless, such justifications are not fully explained by these leaders. This might be due to their emphasis on the pacific nature of Christianity.

MISREADING THE BIBLE

A Christian participant, speaking from the point of view of the side he opposes, explains that the Bible can be used as a pretext to justify violent acts. A Catholic priest stated, "Many people can justify their violent acts by invoking the Bible." According to this priest,

A literal reading of the Bible can justify any act you want it to justify. In the process of justification one may say I must do this [violent act or terrorist act] because this is holy. You can find within Christian scriptures, justification for anything you want to do. There are many Christians who believe that the Christian scriptures must be taken absolutely literally.

A Protestant priest, furthermore, remarks that "99.9% of justifying violence is based on different readings of the Bible. Some people [terrorists] may 'stretch the scripture to justify their own violence.'" Speaking from the voice of the terrorist, he continues:

I think it is possible to read the Bible in such a way as to justify use of force against another country, another religion, or another group. If I can persuade myself that God wants my brand of Christianity, then everything I do will be according to this belief. People may come to that decision, if they read the scripture in a certain way.

Stepping back out of the role of the terrorist, this Protestant priest explains:

I would be certain that any Christian group advocating the use of violence is doing so because they read and interpret scripture in a way that justifies their cause or acts. I think it is stretching the scripture beyond where it could be stretched.

PRO-LIFE JUSTIFICATION

Abortion is a "terrorist act," states a Catholic priest. Catholic interviewees' perceptions concerning this matter of justification are compatible with Catholic role-playing explanations of some violent acts, as in case of anti-abortion violence, that is, Catholics provide almost the same justifications, from both the perspectives of the terrorist and their own. Specifically, a Catholic priest, who is involved in many social activities in addition to his religious duties, gives the following explanation and justification (from the terrorist's perspective) for anti-abortion violence:

You know I truly believe in pro-life choice. Abortion, you know, is violating the rights of humans. I believe that abortion is a terrorist threat, or/and a terrorist act. What is the difference between the right of that fetus as opposed to the right of any other individual in any place? It is still human life. Most of the teaching [in Christianity] preserves the sanctity and the dignity of every human.

Another Catholic priest, when taking the role of the terrorist, compares abortion to capital punishment. He argues:

Capital punishment can be looked upon, by many people, as a terrorist act because it violates the human rights of an individual. But those people do not consider an act of killing in abortion as against human rights of unborn individuals.

While we see that Christian leaders do not accept any biblical justification of terrorism, there is sometimes a justification for the use of violence. Therefore we can see some of the rationale used by Christian terrorists.

Chapter 9

Islamic Justifications

Similar to their Jewish and Christian counterparts, Muslim religious leaders in this study emphasize the fact that their religion, Islam, also is against any type of terrorist acts. According to their definitions of terrorism, Muslim religious participants say that this violence has never been justified in the Islamic faith. In other words, Muslim subjects did not justify terrorism as they identify it. An Imam, Sunni, and full-time preacher in a big mosque, explains this position:

Those who use Islam to justify their terrorism do not represent the Islamic society. Their actions are against our religion, and they are ignorant and misled by others who act against Islam. Their actions provide free service for the enemies of Islam.

Another Sunni Imam goes further and labels terrorist acts in the name of Islam as "Satanic actions," since "Satan tells this kind of people to do terrorism in the name of Islam." Another Imam, with advanced academic degrees from a U.S. university and who serves as a president of an Islamic center, argue: "Islam is against any terrorism and it is the religion of peace." To this Imam:

Islam came to provide security for human beings to live and work in peace. Peace is the ultimate goal of Islam and the true meaning of this religion. A most common Muslim greeting is "Assalam alaikum" [peace be upon you]. The peace and security which Islam provides, are not limited to Muslims, but non-Muslims can also have them. Allah says that if a non-Muslim asks you for security you should do so. So terrorizing other people, Muslims or non-Muslims, is not permitted nor justified in Islam.

Nevertheless, some of the Muslim respondents did approve certain violent acts against, for example, Israeli targets, regardless of the victims of these acts. However, when non-Israeli targets are involved, the approval of the violence would be only against military targets, especially American ones. This kind of approval or justification of violence against Americans is based on the assumption that Muslims and Arabs are in a state of war against Israel, and that the United States supports Israel. This support places the Americans as a major player in the Arab-Israeli conflict. The approval to attack American targets, however, does not cover attacks within the United States. Only violence against

American military targets overseas is justified. None of the Muslim respondents justifies violent acts against "any target" [military or non-military] on the American soil.

Other Muslim subjects, on the other hand, disagree with justifying violence against civilians, regardless of their nationality, and they do not justify violence against American targets anywhere because the United States is not directly fighting the Arabs or Muslims. Thus, in the words of several Muslim religious leaders, "As long as the United States is not involved in any act of war against Muslims, then attacking Americans is not justified." In general, Muslim respondents, as in the case of participants from the other two religions, argue that the use of violence may be justified for certain reasons and in certain situations. Terrorism, on the other hand, can not be justified for any reason found within the Islamic Faith.

The following sections present detailed accounts of the perceptions and attitudes of Muslim religious leaders in justifying violence (not terrorism). Justifications of violence wee centered around specific themes: the use of jihad to fight the "enemies of Islam"; and fighting occupation, especially against non-Muslims. No significant difference was noted between the religious responses of Muslims and their role-playing concerning the belief of what is called "the enemies of Islam." In other words, when Muslim religious leaders are asked to speak in the words of those who do violence in the name of religion, religious leaders often give very similar responses and justifications as to how they themselves would justify violence; therefore there is no need to make any division between their answers.

Regarding violence against other Muslims, many Muslim religious leaders did not accept any justifications for such violence. Specifically, they were completely against it, and there was a difference noticed between their own attitudes and those of the actors' perception.

In short, the perceptions and attitudes of Muslim religious leaders in justifying violence against non-Muslims revolve around the following themes: jihad against the enemies of God; resisting the Israeli occupation; and practicing the right of self-defense.

JIHAD AGAINST THE ENEMIES OF ISLAM (ENEMIES OF GOD)

Muslim respondents provide different justifications for violence against non-Muslims, especially against Israeli and some American targets. All Muslim subjects justify and approve the act of fighting the Israeli occupation in the West Bank, Gaza Strip, and South Lebanon. They considered this kind of fighting justified under the principle of jihad.

However, there is a debate among participants when it comes to violence against Israeli civilians and some American targets. Many do not justify violence against Israeli civilians or American targets within the United States. On the other hand, for many Islamic participants, suicide bombings against military targets can be seen as part of jihad, and therefore are justified violent acts against the enemies of Islam who are in a war situation with

Muslims. For many participants, suicide bombings against civilians (Israelis or non-Israelis) and the 1993 bombing of the World Trade Center in New York are unjustifiable violent acts.

Based on the interviews with the Muslim religious leaders, it is clear that the first and foremost justification of violence in the name of Islam is the principle of jihad. Invoking or appealing to this principle may justify the majority of violent acts against non-Muslims. So, it is imperative to know the meaning of this concept.

One Muslim religious leader, an authority who is well educated in both politics and Islam, states that jihad is commonly "mistranslated" from Arabic to English as "holy war." It "does not only mean a holy war, it has also other meanings." These meanings include self-control, and struggling against desires. Regardless of the problem of translation, religious leaders justify and accept any violent act when it is part of jihad against non-Muslims.

However, an Imam respondent explains that jihad has certain conditions and they must be met to classify an act as jihad. Jihad, or the war for the sake of God and Islam, is the highest noble act a Muslim can perform. Any Muslim who dies in the act of jihad is promised Heaven as a reward for that act. Thus, when the appropriate Islamic authority announces the call for jihad, it is the duty of all Muslims to respond and fight for the sake of God.

An Islamic religious leader, who lived in the Middle East and immigrated to America fifteen years ago, explains the concept of jihad and how it justifies violence against Israel. [His words, as is the case with seven other interviewees, were translated from Arabic into English.] To this participant:

Jihad is a broad topic; it has different types and kinds. It is not only fighting in a traditional war, it can be fighting with words, money, providing weapons to fighters, as well as fighting physically in a traditional warfare. Jihad against the enemies of Islam is very open, and everybody [every Muslim] should sacrifice for the sake of liberating Palestine from the Jews, the enemies of God. Sacrificing for the sake of Islam is the highest moral job for Muslims. God will reward those who sacrifice themselves, and will consider them as martyrs; Heaven is the Place of those martyrs. Accordingly, we must fight to free our land from the Zionist and the American Power. They are the source of all Muslims' and Arabs' problems.

Another Imam, who has a similar background, agrees with the above account but provides different words:

People will not stop fighting Israel with any means, including violent means, because the Israeli Army treats Palestinians badly. So, they have the right to defend themselves. They must fight, according to the jihad principle, and they will lose nothing because they will either gain victory and liberation of Palestine, or they will become martyrs if they die in this fighting.

Jihad, as mentioned, must meet certain conditions. It cannot be an unlimited use of force, violence, or open fighting. One should know what the limits of jihad are. One Imam, who holds a degree in Islamic Law, explains in more detail the principle of jihad and when violence may be justified according to this principle. According to this Imam:

Islam approves some kinds of violence, when violence is the only solution that you have. For example, if you are in a war, Muslims fighting non-Muslims or Muslims fighting oppressors, this kind of fighting is called jihad. But Muslims are not allowed, even in jihad, to kill and target civilians such as women, children, and elderly people. jihad is allowed only in certain cases. For example, when a Muslim country is attacked by another country (oppressor country), jihad is justified for the attacked country to defend itself. Furthermore, jihad may apply when a Muslim country, wherever it is, is attacked by another country and is in need of someone to support it. I stress the fact that it was in need, because if there is no need, Muslims are not allowed to join an offensive war. Like the case of Bosnia, if Bosnians are in need for Muslim help from Pakistan, then jihad is justified for that Pakistani to go and help until they free their country. There is another key element in jihad. That is, only the leader of the Islamic country has the right to announce jihad, and when he announces it, Muslims who are under his rule, or who are subjects to that leader, are obliged by Islam to answer his call. However, there are certain cases in which a call for jihad can be made by non-leaders. For example, when the leader reverts from Islam and becomes an unbeliever. Then, jihad could be announced by a Muslim scholar . . . In sum, jihad is used for defense only, but if you go attack others, this is by no means jihad.

Although this Imam restricts the right to announce jihad to a Muslim leader, when it comes to the Arab-Israeli conflict, every Muslim country has the right to participate in the liberation of Palestine. This Imam says that if a Palestinian leader accepted peace with Israel and did not announce jihad, other Muslims should fight the Israelis, and even the Palestinians, until they free the land, because it is an Islamic land. The Imam explains this point as follows:

In Palestine, the situation is a bit different, because the Palestinians do not have the right whatsoever to compromise a yard of Palestine to the Israelis. If all the Palestinians elect an X-person to be their leader, and this leader accepts the loss of half of Palestine to the Israelis, Muslims should, and will, come to free that other half, and drive the Israelis and the Palestinians out of it, because Palestine is not a national property, but a religious property. All Muslims, all over the world, have the right to determine what to do with Palestine.

Even in jihad certain violent acts are not permitted. As noted, violent acts against civilian targets are prohibited regardless of the goals of these acts. Suicide as a violent act is not justified in Islam either, no matter what the goal of this act is. In this regard, as noted by one respondent, "Muslims are not allowed to kill themselves even for noble goals." An Imam, with an advanced degree in religious education and a long service of preaching in mosques, does not justify the acts of suicide bombers, and considers these kinds of acts as non-justifiable in Islam. However, this Sunni Imam says that he may understand why some people decide to take their lives because of frustration, or because of oppression. The Imam explains Islamic attitudes against suicide as follows:

The rules in Islam are fixed; never kill yourself. The rules also are fixed in Islam concerning when someone is killed. If someone is killed, you have no right to say he is going to Paradise, absolutely not. You only pray for him to go to Paradise. Also, you have no right to claim someone will go to Hell. So, if someone dies, nobody has the ability or the right to claim that he is going to Hell or Heaven. This is a rule of thumb. So, if you say someone is a martyr, what does that mean? It means he is going to Heaven, and that is not acceptable in Islam. Even if a scholar says that, he is going against the rule. This is a rule that has never been given any exceptions. So those people who say that suicide bombers are martyrs, in the first place commit a mistake by claiming someone is to go to Paradise. [Only] the Prophet, peace be upon him, was able to say that someone is going to Paradise. But, these people have no right to say that. So, if a Muslim kills himself, no matter how noble his purpose is, the goals never justify the means. So, if your goal is to take revenge for something you lost, from someone who oppressed you, this does not justify killing yourself, because you are committing suicide. This is suicide, and it is *haram* [not permitted] in Islam. This is prohibited and never allowed in Islam by any of the early scholars.

Despite the fact that this Imam has said suicide is prohibited in Islam, he shows his sympathy with what happens in Palestine. He says that he can understand why some people take their own lives there. He explains:

I sympathize with the situation in Palestine. I feel my family is being oppressed, but I don't have the right to use a bomb to kill myself. However, the situation is very complicated... We have a person who lost his family; some other family members are in jail. He goes to work and is denied work; he grows plants and is denied that too. And after all of that, they [the Israelis] come also to his house and bulldoze it. So, this person loses everything and there is nothing else to lose. In this kind of situation, he decides to do a suicide bombing, or someone in an organization comes to him and tells him: you can do that; you could avenge all that you lost by a bomb which kills so many of the Israelis. Hence, that person gets to kill himself in such a situation.

An Imam from the Shia sect maintains that Islam does not justify suicide bombing against civilians. The Imam continues, "Islam is clearly against killing people indiscriminately. Therefore, I am against that 100 percent. Any violence against civilians is rejected regardless of who carries out that cowardly activity."

AMERICAN INVOLVEMENT IN THE MIDDLE EAST

The majority of the Muslim interviewees explain and justify violence against American military targets in the Middle East because of the American involvement in the Middle East. They consider the American support to Israel and the support to the pro-American governments of Muslim countries as the major two reasons behind this violence. One Imam blames America and Israel combined for "all the problems which the Islamic World faces today." Another

Imam claims that "the majority of Muslims accuse the United States of being hostile to them, either in its foreign policies or in its media."

Therefore, according to this Imam, hating Americans is justified, and he gives the following reason for this hate:

Very few people in the Muslim world can believe that America has nothing to do with the Muslim suffering everywhere in the world. In fact, many (Muslims) believe that America, with its double-standard, with its biased policy, is responsible for the suffering of Muslims. Americans are selective in their reaction to world crises; they are picky when it comes to Muslim countries. So, hating Americans or hating the American government is justified for . . . the differences in the political arena, and the aggression that Americans support against Muslims. The most obvious example of American oppression against Muslims is the unlimited support to Israel. Many other examples are in Somalia, in Bosnia, where America does not pay any attention, but it gives all attention to Kuwait. Why Kuwait, and not Bosnia? That is a double standard. The Americans support any aggression against Muslims by looking the other way, by just ignoring it. They always veto decrees or resolutions that go for Arabs against Israel.

Although this Imam justifies this hate against Americans because of their policies, he does not give any justifications for violence against civilian American targets. Indeed, he considers any violent act, especially within the United States, as terrorism. For this Imam, hating Americans does not justify killing them, and he adds:

Attacks against Americans in the United States are terrorism, and should be stopped, it is not justified by any means, no matter what. Killing someone you do not know for no reason except that you do not like them is not justified; you never know, that person you killed could agree with you against his own government. So when you bomb a building in New York, and you tell others I am bombing it because Americans are oppressing Muslims in such and such country, you cannot justify that through Islam. Do you guarantee that no Muslims are in that building? In fact, you cannot. So it is a totally personal revenge more than a revenge for the nation or the religion. These people claim to be defending the religion, but they are not, they are only using it.

SELF-DEFENSE

Another Imam of the Shia sect justifies attacking American and Israeli military targets in Lebanon, because the United States was part of the Israeli aggression against that country. This justification is based on the right of self-defense. As far as attacking Americans within the United Sates, this Imam accuses the FBI of framing a Muslim group in the World Trade Center bombing in 1993. Nevertheless, he comments that attacking civilian targets is not justified regardless of the target or the specific location of an attack.

This Imam further explains:

The United States continues its unquestionable support, military and financial, to Israel, and protects it against the will of the majority of the United Nations. This is not seen as a terrorist or a violent act. But, when Hizbullah and some Palestinians ask the Iranians for help, so they could defeat the aggressor, Iran is labeled as a state that promotes terrorism, and the others [are labeled] as terrorists. Those who are called terrorists are defending themselves against aggressors. When Israel sends along armored tanks, infantry and aircraft into Southern Lebanon while the world is watching, and is slaughtering many Lebanese civilians—that leaves no option but to fight back the aggression. So, violence there [i.e., in southern Lebanon] is defending yourself against the aggressor. It is a strange world . . . The attacker, who nonstop has bombed Lebanese villages where thousands are driven away from their homes, is not called terrorist while the defenders, who only own simple weapons and try to preserve their dignity, are accused of terrorism.

For another Imam, the only justification for violence, from an Islamic perspective, is in resistance of foreign occupation and in self-defense. This Shia Imam states that it is important to mention that Hizbullah groups have limited their activities against Israeli military targets and never attacked any civilians intentionally. Yet, they did respond to the United States involvement in South Lebanon by bombing the American embassy and some American military barracks. This Imam explains these attacks as follows:

Hizbullah considered the United States at that time as a clear partner to Israel, and American ships did shell southern villages of Lebanon . . . Israel does recognize a state of war with Hizbullah, because in June of 1998 both sides exchanged dead bodies of their soldiers who were killed in attacks against the other. This exchange was based on the law of war, and through the international Red Cross. Thus, Hizbullah is not doing terrorism. It is a state of war with Israel and follows the law of war.

As far as violence in the name of Islam within America is concerned, another Imam, also from the Shia sect, accuses the U. S.'s government of framing some Muslims in the World Trade Center incident to blame Hizbullah, Iran, and the Islamic Palestinian groups. This Imam claims:

Neither Hizbullah nor Iran was involved in any violent act within the United States, especially the [1993] bombing of the World Trade Center [WTC]. The individuals, who were allegedly involved in that act, at one time worked in some capacity with the CIA [Central Intelligence Agency] when they were fighting the Soviet invasion in Afghanistan. But after the mission was finished, the United States stopped its involvement in Afghanistan. It sounds to the rational individual that a deal went badly between this group and their connections in the United States government. It was so cheap to have an Egyptian FBI agent to actually frame the blind Sheikh Omar to approve the bombing of the WTC. By the way, those individuals did not claim this bombing as a religious act and were condemned all over the Islamic World.

VIOLENCE AGAINST OTHER MUSLIMS

Many participants do not justify any violent act against other Muslims, but many of them can give some justifications when they speak from the perspective of those who do violence to fellow Muslims by assuming their role. From that perspective, justifications are centered on the following themes which have emerged from the interview data. These justifications are: Non-Islamic government; corrupted and American-controlled regimes; and implementing Shari'a (Islamic law).

One Imam explains why some Islamic groups engage in violence against their fellow Muslims. He declares that these groups select specific targets within an Islamic country. In many cases "they choose government-related targets, such as official and military personnel, or foreign targets which are associated with the government." The justification from the actor's perspective is that "the country lacks a true Islamic leadership." So, what these groups want is "to replace the current leadership with an Islamic one." Many religious groups believe that "most Muslim political leaders submit to the American ideals." Those leaders "practice unjustifiable submission to the American policy and to the West in general." Therefore, "they do not implement the full Islamic law and that is why many Muslims are suffering in many of these countries." Those leaders also come to power through non-Islamic means. They deprive their people of "basic Islamic democracy and Islamic human rights."

From the terrorists' perspective, the leaders of the West (including both the U.S. and Israel) "work together against any Islamic group or movement and prevent it from reaching power by any means." Thus, attacking these presumably corrupted governments is justified because they denounce Islam's ideals.

Chapter 10

Policy Implications

The final research question focuses on policy issues. The question's focus is on what can be done to deal with religious-based terrorism. In other words, the question put to all participants targeted collecting data pertaining to the countering of religious-based terrorism. Data obtained for this question are divided into two categories based on the themes that have emerged from the responses: first, the steps which can or should be taken before a terrorist act occurs (proactive steps); second, steps which can or should be taken after the act (reactive steps).

In the first category, peaceful steps are suggested by many of the interviewees. These steps include: religious education, good communication between the opposing sides, religious statements that forbid any kind of religious-based terrorism, and political solutions to the conflicts in which religion is being used as a cover for violence.

The participants from the three religions agree that religious education is the best policy in dealing with religious-motivated terrorism. All religious leaders focus on the importance of religious education in their respective institutions. Many respondents believe that the lack of true religious knowledge is the main cause for the use of religion to justify terrorism. All respondents agree, as mentioned earlier, that their religions are against terrorism. This principle should be taught by religious leaders in the various institutions in which they work, and through their roles in society. Religious leaders have a large audience in their institutions; thus, through religious services, leaders can provide education to inform people about terrorism in the name of religion.

In the second category, although most interviewees focus on the importance of dealing with religious-based terrorism before the fact, they also recognize the need to deal with reactive steps with this kind of violence. Issues of punishment and rehabilitation are mentioned as steps to be taken after a terrorist act occurs. Three kinds of punishment emerge from the data: religious, legal, and social. However, the participants consider religious or religious-based punishments more effective in dealing with religious-based terrorists. They recommend this kind of punishment more than other secular punishments because this kind of offender (the religious terrorist) looks for issues beyond this life.

In short, data regarding policy issues are organized according to the aforementioned strata within each religion. The next sections present policy issues (proactive and reactive) from the perspectives of each of the three religions' participants.

JEWISH PERSPECTIVE ON POLICY ISSUES

Religious Education

Many Jewish participants argue for better religious education on the issue of terrorism within their religious institutions, but for some Jewish religious institutions, terrorism is still not an important issue. One Reform rabbi, who remains the head of a large synagogue after many years, says that:

Synagogues are congregations of individuals, and the rabbi serves a number of roles within a congregation. The determination of what are the most important priorities within a congregation really comes from the congregation and not [from] the rabbi. In America, at least at the moment, terrorism for the Jewish community is not an important issue. It is an emotional issue; people certainly respond when there is a terrorist act, and particularly when there is a terrorist act in Israel.

Nevertheless, this rabbi emphasizes the importance of the choice of words which a religious leader might use in talking about any social issue related to violence and which may incite violence. Certain words may motivate other people to commit violent acts because they come from a religious authority. The rabbi argues that "religious leaders have to control their rhetoric and realize that words matter. We should understand the power of words. In the weeks before Rabin was killed, he was called 'Nazi,' 'Pursuer,' 'Traitor,' etc."

Thus, according to the same rabbi, "non-Orthodox rabbis never sanction violence or terrorism in the name of Judaism." This belief, he reiterates, is reflected in the teaching of non-Orthodox synagogues, and many of their followers never sanction this kind of violence. As far as Orthodox Jewish followers are concerned, the above Reform rabbi believes that "it is at times difficult for Orthodox rabbis to speak against other Orthodox rabbis." In other words, the Reform rabbi mentions that "non-Orthodox teachings are directed against any use or justification of violence in the name of religion. Many of those who use violence in this context were from the Orthodox side."

Hence, it is important to control the words, as the teaching of religion in the religious institutions can be employed against using violence and terrorism. Another (non-orthodox) rabbi similarly points out, "People need truly to respect each other through learning about each other. Once that happens, people do not perpetrate violence against each other."

An Orthodox rabbi with ten years of experience, who believes in fighting an open war between two opposing sides but not in the use of terrorism, agrees that terrorism must be condemned and that education might help in this direction. In his words:

There should be one hundred percent condemnation of terrorist acts by religious leaders. Preachers must teach parents so that they can teach their children that terrorism is unacceptable. We should teach [that] in our religion there is no room for terrorists, and we have zero tolerance for terrorists. By teaching and preaching against terrorism, religious leaders can send a strong message to religious terrorists.

This message, according to a rabbi, should include the following:

You [the terrorists] do not operate on behalf of the Jewish people. If you think this is what God intends from you, you are wrong. You are not representing any religious authority . . . And, if we see that you are going to act, we are going to go ahead and stop you. Sending messages to terrorists through education is very helpful when it takes into consideration what the terrorists say to justify their violence. If terrorists claim a certain explanation for their acts, religious leaders should analyze their words and respond to their justification. This is especially true when these justifications contain negative comments or words against others.

A conservative rabbi suggests that we should confront the terrorist's words. He remarks:

Every time somebody says something that is prejudicial or hateful, [it] tends to justify terrorist action. I think this has to be confronted. Religious leaders have the responsibility to stand up for what is true and what is right and which does not take the life of God's creatures. Every human being is made in the image of God. Thus, we cannot justify taking that person's life.

This rabbi goes further and demands a focus on religious education due to the fact that Jews love and seek peace. He argues that "our tradition is always shalom [peace]; that is, we love peace. So these people that use violence are the antithesis of what the religion stands for."

Good Communication

Jewish, as well as Muslim respondents, as in the case of other issues, focus their explanations on the Arab-Israeli conflict. For many of these rabbis, the best way to deal with religious-based terrorism on both sides is to create a mutual and true understanding. However, the problem is in founding mutual trust between the two sides. Each side accuses the other of being aggressive and terrorist. Clearly, good communication between the two parties is desirable to deal with terrorism.

A rabbi with a very strong background on the Middle-East conflict, who has lived in Europe, Israel, and the US, argues for mutual understanding between the two sides. Nevertheless, at the same time he claims that no one can be trusted on the Arab side. He calls for more fighting against the Arab side because all their leaders are terrorists, and he adds:

There has to be understanding between the Arabs and the Jews, a true understanding, and it is very difficult to come to it, because there is no record, there is no representative of the Arab people today. All these leaders [on the Arab side, meaning the Palestinians] are terrorists, and cruel. So, who can you trust? There is nobody to compromise with; there is no organized people, no valid constitution in any of these Arab lands today. So, the only thing you can do is hold on to what you have and fight if necessary, and fight, and fight.

A Reform rabbi, on the other hand, disagrees with the idea of mistrusting the Arab side and he argues for more communication between the two sides. His account is as follows:

As I see the situation now in the Middle East, there will never be a livable peace until there is recognition of the religious motivation on both sides. So both sides need to communicate with each other to reach this recognition.

He suggests searching for similar threads of belief between the two sides: "Look at the commonality that we share with Abraham. There are the roots to find commonality if we choose to. We could use that as a starting point, we need to separate theology from politics."

Religion, according to a Reform rabbi, "is a solution, not a problem in the Middle East." This rabbi argues for a better discourse between Muslims and Jews in the Middle East. He notes that a process of communication has begun in Israel. According to him:

More recently there has been a little bit of that, with a few rabbis trying to build bridges with other religious leaders in the Muslim world. I think that such sincere bridge building among such sincere religious people will do a lot of good. Therefore, I can see religion as the solution instead of seeing it as the problem.

An Orthodox rabbi also emphasizes the need for closer dialogue and searching for commonality between Arabs and Jews to solve the problems through peaceful means. But he reiterates that terrorism should be stopped first, from both sides. If there is no peaceful solution, the rabbi calls for open war, not terrorism, between the two sides. This rabbi perceives the conflict and the solution as follows:

I am going to be honest with you [talking to the interviewer]. I have one demand from the Arab world built upon no terrorism. You [Arabs] want to make war, declare war, fine . . . Let's do it that way, but no terrorism, no hijacking of planes or buses, no suicide bombers, nothing. Having done that, I turn to my Arab brothers and say look, fifty years ago, you were offered a state and you said no. Now, fifty years later, you want a state, sorry, you cannot erase fifty years of history. We have to prove ourselves, and have a period of 20 years, one generation of peace, where you do not teach your children to terrorize. And I will do the same on my side, then we can go to the same situation where in the United States a Jew and a person of Arab descent can sit here and talk. Let us get to that point. I do believe deep down inside that the Jews and Arabs are brothers. We [Jews] recognize Islam as being the only one of the gentile religions that is absolutely monotheistic, and yet we are killing each other; something is wrong with this picture.

Religious Statements

Multiple rabbi respondents suggest that religious leaders should issue formal religious statements against terrorism in general, and against terrorism in the name of religion, in particular. These kinds of statements, they postulate, would help in preventing future terrorism based on religious justifications. A Reform rabbi suggests that religious leaders, Arabs and Jews, convene to issue a statement for their followers. His suggestion goes like this:

I would require, really, some kind of religious gathering, to provide a framework for religious leaders to say: "yes we acknowledge there are chapters and verses in the Torah, and words of the prophets, that could be interpreted as the justification for violence or military action in the name of God. But, in the spirit of peace, we would hope that this would not happen." I think a statement like that, let's say, from the Chief Rabbinate of Israel would begin the process towards peace. And if we could get the religious leaders there [in the Arab side] to come out with statements not to take any more action based on whatever religious codes . . . it would begin the process, and we could sit down and reflect on it.

Another conservative rabbi spoke, with a tone of anger, against the negative role of Muslim religious leaders in dealing with terrorism. He believes that many of those leaders promote terrorism in the name of Islam, and he wants to hear or read a statement from them against terrorism. He gives the following argument on this issue:

I, as an outsider to Islam, say to you, if all of the Imams in the world said that these people who are doing it [terrorism] are against Islam, then I think we would see an end to it. But because so many of your Imams are giving credence and telling people you are going to wind up in Heaven and have all these virtues, it hurts me deeply. Judaism is the opposite. I have been waiting for a religious sheikh or Imam to issue a fatwa that any person who does this [terrorism] is banished from our faith. Most of the rabbis of the world have condemned Goldstein and the man who killed Rabin.

Religious Punishments

The emphasis here is placed on the belief that certain religious punishments should be clearly documented and understood through the efforts of education and the media, that is, a belief that God will punish those who violate His laws in the afterlife. For example, suicide is prohibited in the three religions regardless of the reason; hence, God will not permit killing oneself regardless of the goal of that act. As a policy, this may be used to inform people that there are punishments awaiting those who commit violent acts in the name of religion. The assumption is that religious punishments may deter potential ruthless offenders from future involvement in violence in the name of religion. Arguably, this would be logical because if they know that God will not accept their acts, then they will not engage in such behavior.

One rabbi respondent reasons as follows:

Potential offenders must view the punishments as coming from God. The punishment would have to come with the source, which is God. Religious terrorists would have to be convinced that their punishment would come from an authority greater than us. We could convince them that based on the Bible; God wants peace. I do not think that there is anything we could do to convince an extremist that our [mortal] punishment would deter them from the act based on what they perceive as the will of God.

The rabbi continues to say we can punish those who act out of control based on the Jewish Law. According to that law, "If you operate in a way that is without control, the elders can take you to the main part of the city and stone you until dead."

Nevertheless, this rabbi claims that before the implementation of such a law, we should try other peaceful means with those offenders. He suggests that "every other avenue needs to be explored before we reach the point of stoning. If everything else fails, then we take him [the offender] to the main part of the town and stone him."

In Judaism suicide is a prohibited act. A rabbi explains how Judaism views suicide:

Suicide within Judaism is prohibited and there are whole series of laws with respect to how you deal with suicide. For example, a person who commits suicide cannot be buried in a Jewish cemetery, but has to be buried outside the wall of the cemetery . . . And, you do not have formal mourning for a suicide.

Social Punishments

Religious leaders have called for social punishments for those who engage in terrorism in the name of religion. It is important to communicate to potential religious terrorists, and their organizations, that the religious community will not interact with them because their acts go against religious principles. A Reformed rabbi said, "I disassociate myself from people who would justify terrorism. They are not welcome in the synagogue, and the fact that some people speak loudly should not mean that their point of view is legitimate."

Another rabbi alleges that there is a way to excommunicate one as a social punishment for those who rebel against Judaism. The punishment is called "herem" and derives from the book of Joshua. The rabbi adds, "People under this punishment cannot worship at the congregation; there cannot be any social contact. So, in the self-contained Jewish community, the Orthodox world can have the power of social isolation."

In short, these rabbis assert that social isolation of terrorists can be used as a way to deal with religious terrorism.

CHRISTIANS' PERSPECTIVE ON POLICY ISSUES

From a Christian point of view about policy issues, many respondents share the opinion of the rabbis, especially about the role of education and good communication. It has been noted that there are always common themes between the participants regarding the research questions. However, for the sake of clarification, the researcher divides the responses according to their religions. For Christian participants, the focus is clearly on the peaceful means in dealing with this kind of violence, and they argue that their religion calls for caring and rehabilitation, a theme noted only by Christian participants.

Religious Education

One Catholic priest involved with many social activities, and one who reportedly manages many social problems in the community, blames the social system of the family as being responsible for violent and terrorist acts. Further, he refers to the problem of "freedom of choice," implying that many of our problems are due to the ability of people to possess "free will." He claims that this freedom of choice is "God's mistake." The priest provides the following account:

God's first mistake was [that] he gave us the freedom of choice. And I think that a lot of times we like to blame God for things that go wrong. But it gets down to that basic fundamental principle that God gave us the freedom to choose. And you know, sadly enough, we are the victims of that choice many times, our own as well as the choice of other people. When we look at why an individual views the situation one way as opposed to another, it is a whole family system. How was that person raised? What values were they taught? I believe as long as people are making choices, we are always going to have violence, and we are always going to have terrorism.

This respondent argues that people are making choices based on what they view as good or bad. They have freedom and options to choose from. Thus, they should be taught how to make good decisions. Accordingly, both teaching and good religious education are essential in preparing people to make informed decisions.

One priest states that he advises people not to use religion for their personal gains. He adds, "I believe that many people use religion to their advantage and to their own gain, which is very wrong. You can never hide behind God."

In the future, the focus of education should be on the condemnation of terrorism in the name of religion, all over the world. People should know what their religion says about certain terrorist acts. An Orthodox priest explains:

Let more people know that the church does not condone such acts [terrorist acts]. You cannot talk about the Serbian situation and defend the acts that the Bosnians have done, or for what the Croatians have done either. You cannot defend evil acts. So, there has to be a broad base out there to enable people to realize that anyone who is trying to use the name of the church to further their own ends is acting in sin and is evil. The church does not condone such acts. That would perhaps help pull the teeth out of some of the terrorism that occurs . . . Religious leaders have to speak out more often and more forcefully and that no terrorist act by any group, even by their own, is acceptable. And, get that kind of broad-based understanding of terrorism out to the people . . . so that there would be less tolerance of it.

An Orthodox priest stresses the role of religious institutions regarding social issues such as terrorism and violence. He points to the importance of education in churches, because this education will promote peace and avoid violence. According to this priest:

Churches should take positions on certain issues in society, especially in the case of violence. We can allow education to promote understanding of both sides of a conflict. For example, a church may invite children from both sides in Ireland and give them the opportunity to talk. These kinds of invitations by religious organizations for people from different places can promote peace and avoid violence.

Another priest wants other religious leaders to teach people the respect of human life as a way to avoid violence. He suggests that:

A religious leader, wherever he is, and with whatever group of people he is working with, can help others to learn the dignity and respect of human life. If I truly believe in the dignity of you as a person, then I would never think of overpowering you, or controlling you in any shape or form. I would respect and accept you as you are, and live as brothers.

Rehabilitation

From a Christian perspective, one Orthodox priest views terrorists as victims of their acts and in need of being helped. According to this opinion, society should deal with these kinds of people and try to accept them after understanding their motives and problems; violence against terrorists will not deter them. (No other interviewees, Christians or non-Christians, view terrorists as victims.) This priest argues that:

When we look at acts of extreme terrorists, we are dealing with a small number of people. They are victims as much as they are terrorists. We are always going to have those kinds of people. So we can do our part and leave the rest up to God. That is not despair, or our running away from, or denying . . . it is allowing the goodness of God to touch people's hearts wherever they are. Violence is not the answer for violence.

This priest, though a single voice, suggests a significant theme—that religious leaders may consider talking with these extremists with a purpose in mind; to understand and help the offender. (Thus, he is introducing a medical or a social work model.) This respondent suggests that "this kind of dialogue with the terrorist must exclude any official or governmental involvement, because many of these violent offenders do not trust the government." The priest adds:

Maybe some sort of rehabilitation, if possible . . . maybe there is some way in which to engage them in a kind of conversation that would help them see what they did. Give them chances to understand what religion says, truly, about violence. We should know what was going on in their minds when they did the act. We, as a society, should take responsibility and understand why they are doing this kind of violence . . . The government is not equipped with the necessary means to deal with them [the offenders]; it is the religious leaders' responsibility to deal with them and to listen to what they say. There is a gap of communication between those people and the mainstream.

Not surprisingly, this priest is against legal punishments, especially capital punishment, which he describes as "state violence." But the respondent does not object to enforcing imprisonment for certain periods of time and providing offenders with some kind of rehabilitation. His opinion on legal punishment is very clear, as follows:

I am against capital punishment as a way of dealing with offenders. I believe, to some extent, in imprisonment for certain periods. Capital punishment is state violence, and what makes it better than individual violence?

Legal Punishment

Somewhat contrary to the more therapeutic-minded respondents in the previous paragraphs, some priests consider terrorists simply as "other traditional criminals," who should be specifically punished for their criminal acts. In other words, they believe in enforcing whatever the state's law stipulates for the terrorists' illegal acts. According to a Catholic priest:

Terrorists need to be treated like anybody else who would commit a premeditated act of murder. And I, in line with the principle of the Church, believe that the state has the authority to do certain things to protect society. I would have to support the state's decisions to do as they see fit with terrorists.

Political Solutions

Many terrorist acts are politically motivated. Religion can be seen as just a cover for some of these acts. An argument can be made that if we understand the causes behind terrorist acts, and try to find political and nonviolent solutions, then we may prevent some terrorism. Respondents suggest that the ongoing, terrorist-styled violence in Ireland, the Middle East, and parts of Europe is politically motivated. The solution to this violence, as one priest puts it, is to "understand causes of violence, and find alternatives to violence in dealing with these causes."

Another Protestant priest is more vocal in describing these causes as "buttons of terrorism" which we should not let the terrorists push. He continues:

I would say the vast majority of terrorist acts are seen to be somehow politically based, whether it be militants in Montana that are fighting what they perceive to be an overbearing U.S. government, or whether it be the situation going on in Israel, Palestine, Rwanda, or Bosnia. There is an awful lot of political base to that, an awful lot of nationalism. If the major fires that are going on right now were resolved peacefully, you would probably knock out about 90 percent of the terrorism in the world. We are all capable of incredible violence if the right buttons get pushed.

One Catholic priest argues that religion has the least share of what is going on in Ireland. Other factors need to be addressed when one looks to violence or terrorism in that country.

In Ireland, religion is "a part" of what is going on there. It is more than just religion. It is economic, the social status of society, it is the government that people feel is oppressive to them. I do not know what it is like to be a Catholic in Northern Ireland. I cannot see all the incredible harm and terror that they have to live under.

The point this priest stresses is that one should deal with these other factors when he/she tries to deal with religious-based terrorism in Ireland. Solving these, or many of these problems, would decrease the possibility of using religion to justify terrorism in that situation.

ISLAMIC PERSPECTIVE ON POLICY ISSUES

Religious Education

For many Imams who have participated in this study, the lack of religious education is a key factor which promotes terrorism in the name of religion, that is, the need exists to educate people on how Islam views violence. As one Imam says:

Religious education is what we need in the media, in the Islamic speeches, in the Friday prayers, in schools, and in parenting. Because if we look at the bombers, opinion polls of bombings, you always find that they (the terrorists) were not educated in the ways of Islam. They might hold degrees in engineering, in high technology, but they are not educated "Islamically." They are incapable of explaining what they are doing, or justifying it "Islamically." We need Islamic education that is derived from Al-Quran and from the prophetic tradition, we should say, through the media and all over the world, on what Islam thinks about terrorism.

Good Communication

Respondents believe it is important that Muslims improve their communication with the West in general and explain Islam's position on violence and jihad. One Imam respondent blames Muslims for not being active in this direction. He thinks that

Muslims are not doing their job in explaining who they are and what they stand for. I think Islam is the most misunderstood religion by others. Islam is a great religion and shares many similarities with Christianity and Judaism. It is a religion of peace that does not promote terrorism in any form or shape.

Thus, respondents conclude that through communication Islamic ideas may be placed into their original context. As one Imam stated:

The word "jihad" has been misused by the Western media in such a way as to show that Islam promotes violence. This word has a variety of meanings, the most common of which is the struggle to be a better person, to show self-control, and to be a good servant of God. Yet, the focus [of the media] is not on the peaceful meanings of jihad. The Prophet Muhammad, peace be upon him, describes fighting in a war as a small jihad whereas fighting to be good to yourself, to your family, and to God is the biggest jihad.

Political Solutions

One Imam, of the Shia sect, suggests political solutions to the Arab-Israeli conflict in Lebanon and Palestine. The ideal solution is total Israeli withdrawal from the occupied territories to achieve a lasting peace. The interviewee admits that he used to be against the existence of the state of Israel but has more recently changed his mind, and he now argues for a political solution to the problem. The Imam explains his idea as follows:

I was against the existence of Israel, but I realized it will take many thousands of lives to change the situation. Therefore, I would like to see a peaceful solution to this problem [the Arab-Israeli conflict] in the Middle East. Maybe the best solution is the division of the land between the Palestinians and the Israelis, as it was established in 1948. If Israel returns the occupied land to its neighbor and accepts a peaceful coexistence with the Palestinians, who actually used to own the land and were driven from the land by force, then a long lasting peace could be achieved. Islam emphasizes friendship and love to all people. Muslims lived side by side with the Christians and Jews for hundreds of years. They used to work with each other without any problems and were all protected by Islamic government. There was coexistence with respect to each other's religion. If that was the case in the past, this could be the same in the future, if the parties involved come to a balanced peaceful agreement.

From a different perspective, another Sunni Imam, who approves of HAMAS's actions against Israeli military targets, suggests that liberation of Palestine is the only way to stop violence in the name of Islam. "After that liberation (by any means), Jews can live under Islamic government, because Muslims are fighting the political state of Israel not the Jewish people." This Imam continues:

Our goal must be the liberation of Palestine, all [of] Palestine by any means. So we should get rid of the state of Israel as a political system, but that does not mean that we are against Jews or that we want to throw them in the sea as the Zionists always claim. The opposite is more accurate, we want Jews to stay in Palestine as citizens of an Islamic state and they will have all their rights according to the Islamic law.

Regarding violence against Muslims by some Muslims, political solutions also represent an option to prevent future violence according to many participants. Some Imams ask Arab and Islamic governments to treat their citizens with more respect and give more freedom to their people. These governments should also implement religious laws instead of Western (secular) laws, because the latter contradict Islam. The leaders of these governments should not put their fate in the hands of the West. Then, the best solution is to start a dialogue between these groups and their governments to reach an agreement of how to improve the situation in those countries.

One Imam suggests the following for this kind of terrorism:

For violence or terrorism by Muslims against Muslims, governments and the accused Islamic groups should start immediately a dialogue to find the right solutions. Some of these solutions must include more freedom to the people and giving citizens the right to be involved in the process of decision-making. None of the governments in the Islamic world follow completely "Shari'a," or have a true Islamic system. Our governments should not submit to the policies of the West, because the West does not like Islam and they do only what is good for Israel.

Another Imam also supports the idea of dialogue but refuses any kind of violence against Islamic countries. According to this Imam, violence should not be used as a way to implement religious law in the Arab countries. The Imam adds:

I encourage all sides to sit down and talk to solve the problems. There are some policies in those countries which need to be changed to become consistent with the Islamic law, but using violence to force these countries to change their policies is not acceptable. Change, according to Islam, must start with words through preaching and calling for Islam. Violence will not bring the required change in the Islamic countries; it will bring, instead civil wars. The enemies of Islam will benefit from this violence. Thus, we should focus our efforts to fight those enemies not each other. Hence, the Islamic countries and their opponents should find peaceful solutions to their problems.

Religious Punishments

A primary reactive step must emphasize religious punishment or "fatwa." An Imam participant focuses on the importance of religious punishments by explaining that: "According to Islamic law, the death penalty is permitted in murder cases. The law is very clear by declaring that the offender should be killed." For those convicted as terrorists who have killed other people, "they should be punished by public execution according to Shari'a [Islamic law]." God already declares this punishment, as one Imam notes:

Terrorists may be tried for their crimes by religious judges, and if lives were taken because of their acts, the death penalty is their punishment. Because God says that one who kills a person is like one killing all people, and whoever keeps a person alive, is like one giving life to all people.

With regard to suicide in Islam, many respondents point to the simple fact that "Islam is against suicide, and God will punish those who kill themselves by placing them in Hell forever." Thus, if a suicide act (suicide bombing) is classified as simply suicide, "God will punish the individual who takes his/her life." Nevertheless, there is some disagreement about those who kill themselves in attacks against Israeli and American military targets. Some Imams consider that as a kind of Jihad, and therefore no religious punishment would be forthcoming. Other participants consider it pure suicide and it is punishable by God. In short, the issue of "suicide bombers" is very complicated for many respondents.

CONCLUSION

In conclusion, Muslim participants have not fully elaborated on policy issues. For many of them, what is viewed, by others, as Muslim religious-based terrorism is an act of Jihad in Islam. Therefore, their focus is on justifying violence in the name of Islam as a kind of jihad instead of presenting solutions. According to many of the Muslim participants, as long as a violent act is for the sake of God and against the enemies of Islam, there is no need even to justify or try to stop it. And that is why the answers of Muslims are very short regarding policy issues, unlike those of the respondents in the other two religions.

Reviewing the responses to the three research questions in general, one may notice that Jewish participants were very open and gave more details for the three questions. However, most of their responses were focused on the Arab-Israeli conflict. Christian participants' focus was mainly on policy issues. They gave many details regarding peaceful ways of dealing with violence in many parts of the world. Nevertheless, in the area of justification, the responses were rather short. Muslim participants focused was on the justifications, especially in the case of the Arab-Israeli conflict and the American involvement in the Middle East. Regardless of the length of the responses, one can still make the argument that terrorism according to the three religions is not justified.

One of the interesting findings was that the religious leaders who participated in this study across the three religions recognize and accept certain kinds of justifications for some violent acts. Just war and self-defense, for example, are shared justifications in the three religions combined with the misreading and misinterpretation of scriptures.

Thus, as long as religious-based offenders view their acts as justifiable acts against enemies of God or religion, they will continue to represent a threat to the whole society. This kind of offender justifies and rationalizes acts depending on divine principles. In other words, religious-based terrorism is well justified by different principles, as they were explained above. This process of justification is close to a theory in the field of criminology: Techniques of Neutralization Theory. The relationship between the answers to the research questions and this theory will be explained in the next chapter.

This chapter conveyed the findings of this study and prepared the stage for the theoretical applications. Data were generated from the interviewees, and were organized according to the three main research questions. However, within each research question, certain themes emerged through the process of analysis, as discussed in Chapter 3. Responses from each religion regarding defining terrorism, justifying this kind of violence, and dealing with religious-based offenders were reported. The final section of this chapter explored the relationship between the data and Techniques of Neutralization Theory. The data gave substantial support to this theory since many religious-based terrorists may use one or more of the techniques of neutralization, which will be discussed in more depth in the next chapter.

Part III

Theoretical Understanding

Chapter 11

Theoretical Framework

The author has consulted a number of criminological theories to provide a theoretical framework for this research. It is imperative to understand how religious-based terrorists justify their violence to themselves and to their followers. Therefore, this book has used a predictive theoretical model to serve as a framework for the research questions: First, based on the literature, terrorists want to achieve specific goals, which are not accepted by the majority in society. Second, the goals and the means to achieve them (according to terrorists' beliefs) are not recognized by the formal social control system and in many cases by the society itself. Thus, for terrorists, violence can be viewed as a means to achieve their goals. Mullins (1997) points out that violence for terrorists is "a component of goal-directed behavior. The terrorist is willing to use whatever means necessary to force political [and religious] change, even if this means the death of hundreds of innocents" (p. xii).

As a result, one can make an argument that in religious-motivated terrorism, terrorists try to justify and rationalize their violence to convince themselves first, and the general public second, that their violence is for the sake of God and religion (i.e., for good causes).

Arguably, religious terrorists believe that society is in disarray or a state of confusion, and they aim to change the status quo (which is bad) to a new one (an ideal society). To this end, violence (terrorism) may be used and be justified by religious principles. Accordingly, based on a justification process that may take place in terrorism, one could say that the criminological theory, Neutralization Theory, tends to explain this kind of violence.

NEUTRALIZATION THEORY

According to this theory, many individuals who commit criminal or delinquent acts are able to rationalize their acts as justifiable given a particular situational or cultural setting.

The original idea of neutralization apparently occurred to Gresham Sykes in the 1950s, when he was exploring the relationship among prisoners housed in a large maximum custody prison. The fact arose that prisoners are able to rationalize or "explain away" some of their rule-breaking while within the confines of the prison. Prisoners maintain a rather complex relationship with their keepers. Notably, prisoners locked up under long confinement may devise ways to justify infractions while in the cellblock. The prison itself may be seen as corrupt, making infractions easier to rationalize (Martin, Mutchnick, and Austin, 1990, pp. 304–305).

It must be said that Sykes was well aware of the earlier statement of Edwin Sutherland, that rationalization to commit criminal behavior must be learned along with any techniques for actually violating the law. As Sutherland outlined, but did not elaborate, offenders must learn not only "how to" break the law (techniques), but they must also learn various "rationalizations" which provide a type of personal justification for carrying out the techniques of law-breaking. Hence, many know how, for example, to throw bricks through windows, or to shoplift; but most lack the necessary rationalizations for doing such acts (Martin, Mutchnick, and Austin, 1990, pp. 155–157).

It was not until 1957, with the now highly cited paper "Techniques of Neutralization: A Theory of Delinquency" that Sykes and his coauthor, David Matza, further developed the process of rationalization. The thrust of their argument was to explain how youths tended to justify their rule-breaking and sometimes delinquency. The techniques of neutralization provide no discussion of terrorism. This study, however, extends this theory to include religious-based terrorism within its scope of explanation of delinquent behavior.

It is necessary to review the original ideas behind Sykes and Matza's neutralization processes. These rationalizations are distinct; yet they can be combined with each other with one offender using multiple strategies to justify misbehavior. Also, it may be that some justification techniques are more useful than others for framing a particular kind of infraction. Moreover, it is true that some of the classic techniques of neutralization may reveal relative degrees of absolution (to remove blame from) the perpetrator. That is, some rationalizations may, more strongly than others, place ultimate blame on the victim, for example. Others may argue that the perpetrator realizes his/her guilt, but carries out the misdeed anyway. While in other cases, the perpetrators may not even view themselves as an offenders (thus, purely justifying the act).

Sykes and Matza (1957) devised five types of neutralization.

The Denial of Responsibility

In this case, the juvenile delinquent argues that responsibility is due to factors outside his/her control. For example, "do not blame me, for I was born in a slum and had unloving parents" (pp. 664–670). The list is long, depending on the sophistication of the delinquent who may have sat through many different counseling sessions with psychologists. The youthful law-breaker, for example, learns the language of the social scientists and turns it to his/her advantage. The "outside factors" could be external to the delinquent (such as poor role models or unloving environments) or internal to the delinquent, as in the case of any possible genetic, hormonal, or even nutritional factors.

Likely, in these cases, the youth would admit to guilt but would simply argue the factors that caused the behaviors were outside his/her control. This rationalization may be close to the adage of "society made me do it" or, in the case of physiology, "my own body may be faulty." In this particular technique of neutralization, the offender is not necessarily angry with any specific victim.

The Denial of Injury

Here, the juvenile delinquent rather simply rationalizes his/her infractions by arguing no one was really harmed by the act, even though it may have been wrong. If an automobile is stolen, the youthful delinquents may suggest it was only borrowed for a short time and the vehicle was replenished with gasoline. The car was returned to the exact spot, so who is really harmed? That is, there is "no injury." Perhaps, even "what one doesn't know will not hurt." Gang fighting might be viewed simply as "private quarreling" and of no real concern to the larger citizenry (see Sykes and Matza, 1957, pp. 664–670).

In these kinds of rather unsophisticated rationalizations, the offending delinquents know they are, in fact, breaking the law. In addition, they do not necessarily possess any ill will toward particular victims. The delinquency may be seen as "spur-of-the-moment" pranks which are quickly justified and which do not require the deeper sophistication of the denial of responsibility.

The Denial of Victim

The third rationalization technique presents the argument that the juvenile delinquent believes the victim deserves any harm done. This style of rationalization appears to be more complex than denial of injury. In this situation the delinquent is convinced that he/she is moving into a position of avenger, and the victim, indeed, becomes the wrongdoer. The neutralization is complete to the extent that the infraction is totally dismissed and thus, the concept of "victim" dissolves. This is a case of pure justification and the offender sees him/herself as a Robin Hood-like figure as the crime is rationalized (Sykes and Matza, 1957, pp. 664–670). The offending delinquent is seeking "vengeance" to the extent that any harm is justified. Sykes and Matza refer to this as "rightful retaliation." The illegal act is so justified by the wrongdoing of the victim, that the offender lacks any identification with potential harm. The 1950s cases given by Sykes and Matza may still apply and include: "assaults on homosexuals, . . . attacks on minority groups who are said to have gotten out-of-place, vandalism as revenge on an unfair teacher or school official, thefts from a 'crooked' store owner" (pp. 664–670).

The Condemnation of Condemners

Justification at this point is based on the argument that whoever condemns a violent act, especially the victim, is worse than the offender and therefore is a worthy target.

Sykes and Matza write: "The delinquent shifts the focus of attention from his own deviant acts to the motives and behaviors of those who disapprove of his violations. His condemners are hypocrites in disguise." In this case the delinquent may realize that he/she is committing an illegal act, but is convinced that the accusers are worse. Interestingly, in this case, the delinquent may not be actually seeking revenge but is, nonetheless, able to justify deviance based on the grounds that the potential victim is a worse violator. It may be that this particular style of neutralization may lead to denial of victim, which is more vengeance-oriented.

Examples would include the justification of delinquency due to the fact that police are thought to be corrupt. Alternatively, the juvenile believes that the parent is committing illegal acts, and then the child may justify his/her own deviation. Again, this is a shifting of blame to the accuser, whether the government, society, or even a parent. A child may easily rationalize alcohol abuse if he/she sees parents engaging in the same behavior.

The Appeal to Higher Loyalties

In this technique, the offender claims that he/she is acting for nonpersonal goals, or for the good of others. Thus, in this case, the delinquent will seek altruistic goals which go beyond any personal interests. For example, the youth may show loyalty to a friendship clique or gang and, thereby, rationalize deviance, that is, "going along" with the misbehavior of others because loyalty to the group is even greater than to the law. The noted case of one who steals bread to feed a starving family applies. Sykes and Matza again were emphasizing juvenile behavior as it might apply in school or friendship groups.

APPLICATION TO THE FINDINGS OF THE STUDY

After introducing the theory in its original form, the next step is applying it to the findings of this study. In other words, what is the relationship between this theory and the results of this research? As the findings have unfolded, it has become clear that religious-based terrorists justify their violence in varied ways.

Based on the data regarding justifications from two perspectives, religious leaders as well as the leaders taking the role of the actors (terrorist), it appears that one can logically apply "Techniques of Neutralization" as a theoretical explanation to religious based terrorism.

As reviewed above, this theory is based on five techniques (or rationales) which were thought to have predictive value with regard to the justification of terrorism. Fundamentally, these techniques are indeed found to be useful in clarifying the justifications of religious-based terrorism. As one Christian participant explains, "most religious-based terrorists try to self-justify their violence." The priest continues:

I do believe that there is a self-justification to terrorism. Most people know in their hearts the difference between right and wrong. And with that knowledge, in order to do anything, most people have to convince themselves that it is the right thing to do. The most righteous thing a person can do is to act in the name of their faith. And if you can find justification for an act within the faith, then you can convince yourself that a particular act is right. And if it is right, then you must do it. If you believe something is wrong, you must not do it.

Consequently, many participants concurred that religious-based terrorists find some kind of justification for their violence in order to make it sound. Otherwise, they will not commit this violence. This process of justification may be a self-motivated process, or one which evolves through doctrinal teaching by terrorist groups. Regardless of how they justify their acts, religious-based terrorists tend to use one or more of the five following techniques.

The Denial of Responsibility

Many religious terrorists claim that they are not responsible for their acts. Their acts, they believe, result from external factors over which they have little or no control. For example, Muslim terrorists hold Israel and the United States responsible for violent acts which they carried out as individual Muslims. Because both countries are believed to be oppressing Muslims all over the world, and because they are believed to be responsible for many Muslims' suffering in the Islamic world, action against these oppressors is justified. Thus, the responsibility falls on these two countries and not on the individual Muslim actor.

For Jewish terrorists as well, the responsibility is placed on the Arab and the Islamic world. According to some participants, Arabs want "to get rid of the Jews and throw them in the Sea." Consequently, "Jewish people are responding to Arab violence and terrorism" and the responsibility for Jewish violence must logically be found beyond Jews (as actors) and placed, instead, on Arabs. For Christians the same is true. White supremacists, for example, and anti-abortion advocates consider the American government and society to be responsible for their own violence. They want to solve the problems of American society, but the government is preventing them. In short, religious-based terrorists claim that the other side always holds original responsibility for the violence, because they (the terrorists) are only responding to the wrongdoings of someone else.

It is at this point that the terrorists' view of justification differs, if only partially, from Sykes and Matza's original perspectives. For example, it seems that the terrorist may indeed claim a denial of responsibility but only in reference to "external" factors. That is, the terrorist may claim that the "occupation" of land by an infidel or enemies of religion is, in fact, caused by factors outside the control of the individual (i.e., don't blame me that an infidel is occupying my land). At the same time, it is clear that "internal" factors do not apply in the same sense they did for delinquents in 1957. Thus, terrorists would not commonly try to justify their behavior by resorting to psychological or physiological problems which might unconsciously motivate them toward illegal acts. More likely, it is the case that the more macro-level theoretical assumptions at the political and world level are more relevant as explanatory factors than the micro-level assumptions of the individual's psychology and subconscious drives.

The Denial of Injury

Religious terrorists may justify any wrongfulness of their acts when they deny any real injury resulting from these violent acts. They look to the betterment of society when they consider their violent acts to be a service for the common good, that is, the good outweighs the bad, and, more accurately, the bad is simply rationalized away. Thus, the terrorist denies the existence of injury by focusing on the ultimate "good" which will be reaped by society. Here, there can be seen a type of utilitarian argument which views the ultimate good as certainly more important than any injury. Indeed, this may be an example of the "ends justifying the means."

Also, in the case of denial of injury a distinction must be made between human and nonhuman targets. For example, terrorists might justify their acts by believing that the act was not committed to intentionally kill people (i.e., blowing up an abortion clinic at night when no one is present). There may exist some overlap between this technique and denial of victim. The same argument can be made for both techniques in the case of religious-based terrorism. Clearly, the "just war" rationale, as heavily detailed in the findings, can be subsumed under both of these types of neutralization techniques.

The Denial of Victim

This technique is very clear in religious-motivated terrorism. All interviewees mention that the particular victims in this kind of violence are insignificant or, more pointedly, "out of sight, out of mind" in the eyes of some terrorists. In essence, the individual victim suffers a kind of dehumanization, and the fact that someone loses his or her life is incidental to the act of violence itself. According to their religious goals, as mentioned before, terrorists look down upon any victims as faceless persons who deserve what they get because they are evil in the eyes of the religion. Respondents claim, "some Jews view their victims as 'snakes,' 'outsiders,' and 'evil rotten murderers.' For them God says in the Old Testament that the seven nations in Canaan are 'evil rotten murderous people.'"

On the Islamic side, Imam participants report that some Muslim terrorists view those same Jews as "nonbelievers," "evil," "monkeys," "enemies of God and Islam," and "occupants who torture innocent people." Thus they explain: God mandates killing those Jews and reward will come in the life after. It is jihad to fight, to liberate the Islamic land which is under occupation, so you have the right to defend it and liberate it by any means. Accordingly, there is total "denial of victims" for terrorists on both sides of the Arab-Israeli conflict.

Christian terrorists also deny that any kinds of victims resulted from their violence. Victims "deserve to be attacked," for example, because they are non-whites in the case of the KKK, which looks at minorities, Jews, and non-whites as less than human. For anti-abortion groups, those "who perform abortions are murderers and they must be punished."

Here the offender rationalizes the illegal activity by believing that the victim deserved what he/she got. All terrorist groups and organizations subordinate and denigrate victims, and they believe that the victims, as targets, deserve the violent action against them. For some groups, bombing or killing government officials is justifiable because those victims work in a bad system. To other groups, attacking specific targets that represent particular ethnic or racial groups is not a crime because the targets need to be taught a lesson.

In regard to denial of victim, it is clear that the early works of Sykes and Matza apply. The perpetrator of terrorism, just as in the case of the delinquent, is convinced that retaliation is appropriate and necessary. Indeed, the Robin Hood concept can apply in both instances. Perhaps, for example, "attacks on minority groups" in the 1957 example of Sykes and Matza can now be applied to the right-wing religious terrorists who attack certain non-white people in the United States in the name of Christianity. It is critical to realize that in this case, the offenders do not in fact view themselves as being deviant, but rather purely exonerated due to the act promoting a form of "rightful retaliation or punishment."

The Condemnation of Condemners

This technique is explained in the case of defining religious-based terrorism in the findings for the first research question. Each side of opposing terrorist confrontation condemns the other and refers to the other as "terrorists." All parties in any religious conflict consider the other side as being the "infidel," in a wrong position, and performing acts which must be condemned. Some Jews label any violence from the Arab side as terrorism, and the opposite is true when viewed from the Arab side. Some Muslims condemn the United States because of its support to Israel and define both countries as states supporting terrorism. Perpetrators of anti-abortion violence condemn their opponents and label them as murderers and sometimes terrorists. Even if one side in a conflict were to admit that they were engaging in violence, they would always proclaim that the enemy or the "infidel" is engaging in worse or more evil activity, thus further rationalizing their own activity even if such activity is technically wrong.

In this case, the relevance to delinquency is also clear. Both the delinquent and the terrorist will argue that they may be committing illegal acts, but the victim is actually engaging in worse activity. Thus, the delinquent and the terrorist are "shifting the focus of attention from their deviant acts to the motives and behavior of those who disapprove of their acts" (see Sykes and Matza, 1957, pp. 664–670).

The Appeal to Higher Loyalties

In the case of religious-motivated terrorism, this particular technique is basically self-explanatory. God and religion are the higher authorities to which terrorists appeal. Some terrorists, as noted in the presentation of subject accounts, often aim to please only God in their violent acts. Sometimes it may be a kind of sacrificing of oneself for the sake of God and religion. Such terrorists can take words literally from Holy Scripture and interpret such words in ways that justify their violent acts. Jihad, maintaining the land of Israel, and protecting society, or preventing future violent acts, and all the justifications which have been mentioned in the findings chapter, are concepts that terrorists can appeal to as higher authorities. This category of justification by a higher authority can also be easily borrowed from delinquency theory as used by Sykes and Matza. Additionally, all religious-based terrorist acts are justified in the name of God and religion. Religion is seen as the only acceptable moral system and, through it, terrorist acts are rationalized.

To conclude, in justifying religious-based terrorism, the findings of this research give fundamental support to techniques of neutralization as a theoretical explanation for this kind of violence. By considering religious-based terrorism, conceptual clarity is given to the various styles of neutralization as originally outlined by Sykes and Matza in 1957. However, it appears true that, upon reflection, the weakest of the techniques—as applied to terrorism—is the "denial of responsibility." It is clear, for example, that the internal elements of responsibility do not apply and some terrorist organizations or groups take responsibility for their violent acts. The particular relevance of "denial of responsibility" deserves further scrutiny.

In addition, these techniques tend to occur before commission of the criminal or deviant act. They serve to motivate or facilitate deviation by providing justification for the citizenry to violate societal norms. Once one is able to neutralize the violation of social norms, one is free to drift into lawbreaking. Much terrorist literature discusses how individuals must be socialized or conditioned (reeducated) to be able to rationalize their deviance or criminality. Many terrorist organizations hold special training camps, which indoctrinate members to various techniques of rationalization. Those techniques help terrorists to justify their means until they achieve the intended goals; then they will design their own goals and means according to their interpretations of religion.

It is critical to place this kind of violence within a theoretical framework to be able to better understand and ultimately resolve such violence. This study does not finish the discussion of how religious-based violence might be justified, but only sheds some additional light on an old topic. More precise and actual testing of the fundamental theory of neutralization may soon be in order. Also, over the course of the project, it has become clear that the potential for viewing the various techniques as being hierarchical in order deserves additional exploration. It might be shown, for example, that one type of neutralization presumes the existence of another, possibly lower in the hierarchical order of techniques. Additionally, the kind of theoretical research portrayed here helps to isolate themes regarding religion and terrorism which might be given quantitative analysis, should survey research be conducted. Religious-based terrorism continues to be a relatively unexplored research area in criminology. Accordingly, more application of criminological theories to explain terrorism is timely and needed.

Chapter 12

Conclusion

To conclude, it is necessary to examine observations on religious-based terrorism resulting from the attitudes and perceptions of the religious leaders who participated in this study. It is understandable, as mentioned in the methodology chapter, that generalizing these data to larger populations would be inappropriate, or at best should be made with extreme caution. Based on the presentation of the data as manifested in the previous chapter, a number of theoretical propositions may be induced which can be useful in future research. Moreover, the data presentation chapter and the interviewee accounts in response to the research questions provide bases for outlining a number of policy recommendations which are set forth in this chapter. The chapter reports conclusions related to the research questions, and based on these conclusions, some policy and research recommendations are given.

REGARDING DEFINITION

In reference to the first research question, this study failed to arrive at a single, unified definition of terrorism in the name of religion. This finding mirrors the literature regarding the difficulty of defining terrorism.

Participants gave varied responses about how we should define terrorism. As mentioned in Chapter 2, there are more than one hundred definitions of terrorism in the literature. No single definition has ever been reached which enjoys the agreement of all scholars and cultural areas of the world. This study corroborates the extreme difficulty related to defining terrorist violence.

Nevertheless, this study has found common themes that may be useful in defining terrorism. Accordingly, one can propose the following definition, based on the data collected in this study, which appears to be the closest to a unifying meaning regarding terrorism in the name of religion. *Religious terrorism is a violent act against others (individuals, groups, or states) to coerce them to behave or act according to the perpetrator's (individual, group, or state) interpretation of a religion.*

By applying the proposed definition to religious-based terrorism, as mentioned in the previous chapter on presentation of data, one can explain and understand the following cases of terrorism. For Jewish terrorists, their misinterpretation of their religion motivates them to act violently to force their religious belief on others. For those terrorists, Arabs should leave the land of Israel in order to create a pure Jewish state and to gain full control over the land. The religious idea behind this goal is that non-Jews should not control any part of the land of Israel. Thus, violence might help achieve this goal by creating fear among Arabs, which in turn may lead them to leave the land. The perpetrators of this violence do not define such action as terrorism, and instead define the Arab's violence as terrorism.

On the other hand, Arab and Muslim terrorists view Jews in Israel as occupants, oppressors, and enemies of Islam. They do not refer to their Muslim-perpetrated violence as terrorism. To the contrary, they consider the Jewish violence as terrorism. Muslim-terrorist groups try to achieve a religious goal: the creation of an Islamic state in Palestine. Therefore, they feel it is a religious duty to eliminate the state of Israel and to establish their own Islamic state between the Jordan River and the Mediterranean Sea. However, they accept Jews as citizens within this new Islamic state. For these Muslims, violence and fighting against the state of Israel is a religious mission, because Palestine is an Islamic property and should remain under Islamic rule. In short, in the Arab-Israeli conflict, each side accuses the other side of being terrorists.

Violence is defined as terrorism by both sides in a non-traditional way, that is, each side defines the violence of the other side as terrorist. But, for the extremists and terrorists on both sides, violence is justified in order to implement religious ideals, and to force the other side to accept their version of religious misinterpretation.

The case of Muslim and Jewish violence is similar in some ways to that of Christian violence in the United States. For some Christian terrorists, the white race must control the country, and non-whites must be thrown out of the country. According to some Christian respondents of this study, such a call for white power and control is not within the Christian belief, though. Those who use violence against abortion clinics, on the other hand, are trying to implement their interpretation of Christianity by force, and to claim that they are "pro-life" advocates. In other words, Christian extremists use religious goals to justify their violence and do not consider their acts as terrorism.

Defining terrorism depends upon which particular cultural base you are standing on and for what particular goal this definition may be attempted. However, the definition proposed in this study is based on the common elements of the interviewees' definitions of terrorism. The proposed definition accounts for violence in the name of religion regardless of its perpetrators, whether they are groups, individuals, or states. Hence, the current violence in the three religions is defined as terrorism according to the proposed definition, which is based on the religious leaders' perceptions and attitudes in defining terrorism. Many participants in this study defined certain religious-based violent acts as terrorism regardless of the perpetrator, goal, or victim of that act.

REGARDING JUSTIFICATIONS

In reference to the second research question, which focused on the justification of religious-based terrorism, participants responded in varied ways, each from his particular religious perspective. Nevertheless, many religious leaders from the three religions agree on the following areas in which violence (not terrorism) may be justified: The case of a Just War; Preventing future violence; Self-defense; and Controlling the land.

The Case of a "Just War"

According to responses of religious leaders from the three religions, a "just war" is an acceptable justification of violence in the name of religion. Although Muslim participants did not use the term "just war" in their justifications, the concept of Jihad is very similar. However, as mentioned in Chapter 4, the three religions assure that certain rules and conditions must be followed and met in fighting or declaring a just war. A main factor is that the end goal of this war should be achieving peace in order to justify the killing of some people in such a war. Nevertheless, efforts must be made so as not to cause harm to innocent and civilian people, even in a just war (specifically, no intentional harm to civilian and innocent people).

Preventing Future Violence

This justification could be used to deter the enemy or the opposing side from using violence. This is evident in Judaism and Islam especially in the case of the Arab-Israeli conflict in Israel, the West Bank, and Lebanon. Both sides of the conflict claim that their violence is to prevent the other side from inflicting violence. Thus, offenders from both sides justify their terrorism according to this principle and simply claim that they are responding to their opponent's violence.

Self-Defense

Justification of violence for the purpose of self-defense represents a most fundamental rule in all of the three religions. All participants agree that violence under this rule is acceptable if it is the only means for self-defense. Thus, it is acceptable to use any violent means to protect one's life and others' lives if violence is the only way to save these lives.

Maintaining Control Over the Land

This justification was noticed among Muslim and Jewish respondents. Both explain this kind of justification from a religious perspective. For Jews, the land of Israel is holy and every Jew must maintain the power over this land. Thus from a theological perspective, it is a violation of religious law to give away this land to non-Jews. It is a duty of every true believer to protect this land. For Muslims, on the other hand, if Islamic land comes under occupation by a non-Muslim state, all Muslims are required to fight against this occupation until the so-called aggressor leaves the land. That is the case in the West Bank and Lebanon, and it was the case in Afghanistan during the 1980s. In other words, jihad is the only way, from a religious perspective, to free the occupied land from its occupants if political means failed.

Despite any differences between the respondents regarding justifying violence in the name of religion, one can safely isolate the following themes as reasons for why some people resort to religion to justify their violent acts, according to the interviewed religious leaders' points of view:

1.   Misreading and/or misinterpretation of a doctrine (i.e., literal interpretations, reading religious verse out of context, and selective understanding of the religion).
2.   Frustration with status quo.
3.   Looking to achieve certain goals. These are: Political goals, which include, for example, either the creation of a state in Palestine, Ireland, and the U.S., or defending the state as in the case of Israel; Social goals, which are exemplified in racial domination in the U.S., or full Jewish control in the West Bank; or purely religious goals represented in implementation of religious laws in the Islamic countries, enforcing Jewish laws in the land of Israel, or controlling family issues according to Christianity as in the case of violence against abortion.

REGARDING POLICY

The third research question relates to policy issues. All participants argue in favor of steps to be taken before the act of terrorism or violence is carried out (i.e., pro-active steps). Religious education and good communication are the most important steps recommended by the participants. Religious education should include what the religion itself dictates about terrorism. Since all interviewees mention that their religions are against terrorism, they should include this position in their preaching within their respective religious institutions.

This process may be directed to people who attend services in the religious institutions, and/or to a general audience through media, workshops, or conferences.

Moreover, religious leaders should issue statements against terrorism in general, and against religious-based terrorist acts: That is, after a terrorist act, religious leaders should convene and issue a statement to condemn the act, and to explain how this act is not justified by religion. The assumption is that such religious education may reach those who believe in, and justify, terrorism in the name of religion. When these people listen, read, or know about the real religious position on terrorism from well-respected religious leaders (not affiliated with a government and without government titles), then those individuals may challenge their own organizations and groups.

Good communication between religious leaders and groups who are involved in religious-based terrorism represents another important issue in dealing with this kind of violence. Communication can be initiated first within each religion (intra-faith dialogue) and then across religions (inter-faith dialogue). In each religion, a dialogue between the extremists and the mainstream religious leaders may be established. The goal of this dialogue should be to reach a mutual understanding about the relationship between religion and terrorism. After that, another kind of dialogue should be maintained between religious leaders from the three religions (inter-faith dialogue) for the same goals. The outcome of this dialogue may enhance religious education, and it may help control the extremists without any official intervention.

During this dialogue, government-affiliated religious leaders or institutions should be excluded because many of those who believe in violence in the name of religion do not trust their governments. Many of those extremists feel that their governments are far away from the "true" religion. Thus, at the initial stages, dialogue could start from neutral religious leaders within the religion and from other religions. Interviewees in this study encouraged this kind of dialogue.

However, religious leaders in this study did not exclude the possibility of reacting after a terrorist act has occurred. All participants believe, to some extent, in punishing terrorists, but many religious leaders consider traditional legal punishments to be ineffective with regard to religious-based terrorists. For these offenders, legal punishments, even the death penalty, will not deter them because they often look for religious rewards from their God after death. As long as their acts are acceptable to God, these offenders do not care about any punishment inflicted by human beings. How does one punish a person who goes smiling to his/her death? Suicide bombers, for example, go to their deaths to achieve rewards from God in the life after. Thus there is no apparent legal punishment to deter this kind of offender. But the same offender may show fear from religious-based punishments. Many religious-based terrorists will be deterred from any punishments coming from or approved by a scripture. For example, suicide is a forbidden act in the three religions, and whoever commits this act will be punished in the life after. Even in this life there are some kinds of punishments for those who kill themselves, such as the knowledge that they may be denied a place in the same cemetery with those more faithful followers of the same religion.

As a result, to inflict effective punishments upon religious-based terrorists, those offenders must view these punishments as religious ones. If they know that their acts are punishable by God, or that legal punishments are approved by God, they will more likely be deterred.

RECOMMENDATIONS

Policy Recommendations

The most important finding related to policy issues, the focus of the third research question, is the inter-faith dialogue between religious leaders in the three faiths: That is, dialogue within each religion and dialogue between the three religions. As a result of this inter and intra-faith dialogue, terrorism as a concept must be defined, based on the common elements shared by the three religions. After that, a joint religious statement (fatwa), by followers of the three religions, could be issued to clarify terrorism in the name of religion. This statement should make it forbidden and "haram" (a Hebrew and Arabic word) for anybody (individual, group, or state) to use religion to justify any terrorist act. This statement should be publicized through media, conferences, and religious institutions. This statement may shake the belief of those who are active in religious-based terrorism and may prevent potential terrorists from joining these groups. The higher the ranks of the religious leaders who sign the statement, the more impact it may have on terrorists.

This statement should come from religious leaders who are not affiliated with any government positions to avoid the impression that terrorism is a political matter. A purely religious conference for leaders from the three religions may have the effect of discouraging people from engaging in terrorism. By following these recommendations, we may control the supply side for terrorist organizations. Based on this author's personal experience in counterterrorism, many religious-based terrorist organizations rely on religious leaders and institutions to recruit members for their violent activities.

Effective and continuous communication between religious leaders from the three religions, preferably non-government leaders, through media, conferences, and workshops will support the religious statements against terrorism. In other words, an ongoing process, rather than a one-shot dosage, of condemnation of terrorism is needed. This process of communication may be extended to include religious leaders from groups and/or organizations which support violent acts in order to listen to their side of the story and to start an open dialogue with them to explain what is the real position of religion about violence. Again this kind of dialogue must start first within respected religious organizations between high-ranking spiritual leaders.

Research Recommendations

The findings and analyses of this study allow one to make an argument for future research to test the following assumptions, which were deduced from data generated from the interviews as presented in the findings chapter. Testing the following assumptions with different kinds of samples and in different places should allow for a better understanding of religious-based terrorism. One also can make comparisons between perceptions and attitudes of religious leaders from different regions of the world to see if the location has any impact on their responses.

The recommended assumptions for further research include:

1. Relying on literal interpretation of a scripture, with the approval of a religious leader, represents the fundamental precondition for a religious-based terrorist act to be committed.
2. Appeal to God and religion is a foremost justification for religious-based terrorism, and it includes a denial of victim (i.e., victims being viewed as enemies of God and religion).
3. Political, not purely religious goals, are what many current religious-based terrorists try to achieve in the name of the three religions (Judaism, Christianity, and Islam).
4. Religious education through statements and the media, is the most effective policy for dealing with this kind of violence.

Research on religious-based terrorism should be conducted in the United States and other places. This study would be enhanced, and/or findings may differ, if religious leaders from diverse world areas are interviewed and compared with religious leaders within the United States. Further research is called for to better understand this phenomenon and its influence on traditional terrorism.

Appendix: Methodology

This section details the process of collecting the primary data of this book. It comprises the following sections: research questions, research design, population and sample, in-depth interviews, interview guide, data collection procedures, data analysis, validity and reliability, limitations, and human subject's protection.

RESEARCH QUESTIONS

The purpose of this study is to investigate the relationship between religion and terrorism. Three broad areas were covered regarding this topic: a definition of terrorism in the name of religion; reasons and justifications for such terrorism (theoretical issues); and issues pertaining to the possible ways of dealing with this kind of violence (policy issues).

Stated more specifically are the following precise research questions, which provided a framework for this study: First, how does the perception of terrorism differ between leaders of the three religions? Second, what are the religious leaders' attitudes and perceptions regarding justifications of selected terrorist acts? Third, what are the perceptions and attitudes of religious leaders that may promote or discourage selected terrorist acts? That is, what specific roles might religious leaders play to reduce or promote terrorist activity?

The above questions deal with thoughts, beliefs, attitudes, and perceptions. Thus, this study is qualitative in nature as opposed to quantitative.

RESEARCH DESIGN

The purpose of this study is to explore, as well as understand, the relationship between religion, as an independent variable, and terrorism as a dependent variable. Given the nature of the intended purpose, a qualitative approach was found to be most suitable to employ since we are dealing with the perceptions and thoughts of the participants. Qualitative research is a "systematic, empirical strategy for answering questions about people in a bounded social context." Moreover, "it is a means for describing and attempting to understand the observed regularities in what people *do*, *say*, and *report* as their experience" (Locke, et al., 1993, p. 99, emphasis added).

In this approach, the researchers deal with the words of the participants by which they describe their feelings and explanations of events. Researchers treat these feelings and explanations as significant realities (Looke, et al., 1993). For these reasons, a qualitative approach suits this kind of inquiry more than a quantitative one.

The study provides rich descriptive information regarding religious-based terrorism and its justification. F. Hagan (1993) argues, "descriptive research attempts to accurately describe or characterize individual or group's attitudes, behaviors, or characteristics . . . without attempting to examine causal connections" (p. 61). The project examined the relationship between religion and terrorism from the religious leaders' perspective. Consequently, the researcher was not searching specifically for frequencies, distributions, or numerical data on particular variables of a population. Instead, what he sought were the specific words and interpretations of the spiritual leaders. It was fully anticipated that the descriptive narratives provided by the religious leaders would yield a series of case studies. Such cases allowed for an analysis of the research questions, although from insightful personal accounts rather than from quantitative assessments.

POPULATION AND SAMPLE

The conceptual population of this study includes religious leaders of the three traditional religions in the United States. It is a widespread population, found in almost every town and region throughout the country. Thus, it was very difficult to identify each element in this population to be selected in the sample. Hence, the researcher was not able to draw a true random sample from this population. Such an attempt would have required a master list of the conceptual population under investigation (Mutchnick and Berg, 1996). Also, the sample cannot be truly a random one in an interview-oriented design, because the interviewee must consent and, in many cases, sign a consent form. This process affects the true randomness of any sample, because the necessity to replace those who do not consent requires another process of selection.

Keeping in mind the requirements of a true random sample, and the limits of time and resources, the researcher relied on a non-probability, untrue random sample (i.e., purposeful sample). For the purposes of this study, religious leaders who were selected in the sample were persons identified as the official spiritual authority employed in a religious place for worship that included synagogue, church, or mosque.

The sample includes religious leaders from each of the three religions as well as the primary sects in these religions. The researcher has considered a range of religious sects within each religion in order to represent the population of religious leaders and to maximize the possibility of looking at a wide spectrum of perceptions of religious-based terrorism. In short, it is a purposeful sample.

R. Mutchnick and B. Berg (1996) argue that a purposeful sample requires the researcher to have knowledge or expertise about the intended population, and then to select the participants to represent this population. Since the purpose of this study is to explore and understand the perceptions of religious leaders toward religious-based terrorism within the United States, the sample of this study was drawn from the available number of those leaders in the research setting.

A stratified, purposeful sample was selected for this study. Through lists of religious organizations and telephone directories, a list of many religious centers was compiled. Besides this method, the researcher asked for help from informants to locate potential participants for this study. Twenty-four religious leaders from the three religions composed the final sample.

The process of selecting the sample was based on several criteria:

For Jewish participants, the researcher relied heavily on the help of friends and informants. The researcher strove to recruit participants who represented the three major sects within Judaism: Orthodox (traditional), Conservative, and Reform. Therefore, three participants (rabbis) were chosen to represent each sect within this religion.

Regarding Christian participants, three major sects were also represented in this study: Protestants, Catholics, and Eastern Orthodox Christians. Three religious leaders (priests) from each sect were included in the sample.

Muslim leaders represented the third group of participants in this study, and included two major sects, Sunni and Shia. Four Imams/sheikhs were chosen to represent the Sunni sect, but only two Imams from the Shia sect were included in the sample; it was very difficult to recruit participants from this sect.

The sample, according to the aforementioned criteria and strata, was chosen to closely represent the population. The researcher makes no claim that the sample was representative, in statistical terms, of religious leaders in the United States. However, it was diverse enough to provide significant data in response to the research questions of this study. After selecting the participants and following subject protection procedures, to be discussed later, the researcher conducted in-depth, subjectively-oriented interviews.

IN-DEPTH INTERVIEWS

The researcher collected the primary data for this project through highly in-depth, subjective, face-to-face interviews. This process of in-depth interviewing enables researchers to understand the perceptions of participants, and it enhances the ability to learn how people construct meanings of their experience (Berg, 1995; Seidman, 1991).

The in-depth interviews represent, at least in part, conversations rather than formally anticipated and structured questions. "An interview is a method of data collection that can be described as an interaction between the interviewer and the interviewee to obtain valid and reliable information from the participant's view" (Marshall and Rossman, 1989, p. 82). Moreover, interviewing is a useful way to collect data quickly, to follow up questions, and to clarify the data (Marshall and Rossman 1989; Berg, 1995).

Because terrorism is a sensitive topic, in-depth interviewing provides the most valid data-gathering procedure. E. Babbie (1990) identifies the following advantages of using interviewing as a research method:

First, the presence of the interviewer has major impact on the data collection process (i.e., especially in rapport-based interviews). It is easy for a participant to ignore a mail survey involving a sensitive topic compared to an interviewer prepared to engage in an actual conversation.

Second, the interview process allows the interviewer to ask the participants for detailed information and further clarification. This is not available in questionnaire-styled procedures. As this study deals with a very complicated issue of terrorism, the possibility of misunderstanding some questions and of miscommunication can be expected. Therefore, interviews, as a method, will allow the researcher to clarify for the participants any potential confusion, which helps, in return, to obtain clear responses.

Third, in-depth interviewing allows researchers to adapt to different situations of each interview. In this study each religion, and each sect within each religion, has its unique ways and unique points of view for dealing with the topic of this research. Religion X, for example, predictably will differ from religion Y in defining, or dealing, with terrorism. The subjective, rapport-oriented interview process allows these differences to be explored in depth. This advantage is not available for mail or self-administered surveys or scaling procedures.

Moreover, the possibility of using probing questions (e.g., "tell me more," "how come," "what do you mean," etc.) in interviews permits researchers to obtain responses from interviewees not available in fixed-response instruments. C. Marshall and C. Rossman (1989) argue that by using immediate probing, interviews are useful in gaining in-depth answers and a large quantity of information. It was very important in this study to obtain as much detail as possible about terrorism, and the use of probes was critical toward this end.

This researcher acknowledges that some disadvantages also apply to the use of interviews. It has been said that there is no perfect research, and Hagan (1993) says further that the only perfect research is no research. Many researchers point to the fact that interviews may be very time-consuming and costly (e.g., Mutchnick and Berg, 1996; Berg, 1995; Rubin and Rubin, 1995; Hagan, 1993).

Another disadvantage of using interviews is the possibility that interviewees may not be willing to share their information with the interviewer, or the interviewer may not ask the right questions due to the lack of expertise

(Marshall and Rossman, 1989). This researcher understands the disadvantages of interviews and made constant attempts to overcome these problems. Also, attention to these problems not only helps to control them, but also works to enhance the validity and the reliability of data collection. (More details about controlling disadvantages will be introduced in the section on validity.)

Moreover, the researcher used an interview guideline to control the potential disadvantage of not asking the "right" questions. This guide was checked (pre-tested) with peers, professors, and religious people (not from the sample) for ambiguity or the absence of important questions about the topic. In addition to the questions in the interview guide, constant probing used by the researcher worked to assure that sufficient depth was gained in any particular question or theme. Many disadvantages were minimized by (a) using the interview guide to ask the right questions, and (b) by encouraging the participants to talk and share information with the researcher, augmented with high levels of rapport.

INTERVIEW GUIDE

The study used semi-structured but in-depth interviews. Therefore, the researcher used a pre-constructed interview guide with specific, semi-structured questions. Questions focused on the perceptions of the interviewees, and no personal or sensitive questions were asked regarding any direct involvement in illegal or terrorist activity: that is, information was sought regarding how religious leaders *perceive of* religious involvement in terrorist activity, *not* their direct knowledge of any specific involvement.

The interview guide served as the framework for asking questions in the interview sessions. This guide consists of questions to elicit data to answer the three major categories of the research questions.

For the first category of research questions which deals with defining terrorism, the following specific questions were used in the interview guide: How is violence perceived in your religion? In your religion what kinds of violence, if any, may be permissible? Please tell me in detail about your own perception of terrorism. In other words, what is terrorism from your religious perspective? Do you believe some people commit terrorism in the name of religion? How does the religion you represent manage such a possibility? Does your religion have a particular doctrine or official view of terrorism?

The second category of research questions involves reasons for, and justifications of, religious-based terrorism. The following questions in the interview guideline were used to collect data that answer the research question: According to the sacred writings or principles of your religion, can terrorism be justified? If so, how? How do you interpret the concept of "holy war" in your religion? What kinds of victims, based upon the ideology of your religion, may deserve this kind of violence? Some people commit suicide (e.g., suicide bombers) in the name of religion and kill other people. How does your religion perceive this act? In the perception of people of your religion, why do you think some of them commit terrorist acts in the name of their religion? What kind of rewards might they receive because of these acts (based upon your religion's principles)? Do you believe some religious doctrines provide justification of terrorism? Why might this be? What would you say about the views of other religious doctrines (other than your own) about terrorism?

The final category of research questions targets certain policy issues which may exist in the religious doctrines concerning terrorism. To this end, the interviewer used the following questions in the interview guide to answer this research question: Religious leaders are well respected in their communities. What role, if any, can they play in educating others about the issue of terrorism? What is your perception of the relationship between people of different faiths regarding terrorism (e.g., inter-faith dialogue, conferences, peace workshops, and print publications)? There are many religious organizations all over the world; what role can, or should, these organizations play in dealing with terrorism? Based upon religion, what should happen to terrorists if caught? Should they be punished?

This interview guide represented only semi-structured questions. The interviewer inserted probe questions such as "why?" "why not?" "how come?" or "can you elaborate?" whenever it was necessary during the interview session. In some cases, and as part of the more in-depth probing process, the researcher interjected specific and highly publicized terrorist events. He asked the interviewees how their religions tend to respond to such events (e.g., anti-abortion acts; World Trade Center bombing; Oklahoma City bombing; the assassination of Yitzhak Rabin; suicide bombers).

To summarize, the interview guide helped the researcher to: (a) focus on the research questions during the interview session; (b) encourage participants to talk about the topic under investigation (because it gave them areas to start in which they could share their information with the researcher); and (c) provide certain themes and categories for the analysis and interpretation stages of the project.

DATA COLLECTION PROCEDURES

After selecting the participants, the second step was to obtain their voluntary approvals to be interviewed. The researcher contacted many potential participants by phone (or through personal contact) to arrange the first meeting. In this meeting, the researcher explained, in detail, the purpose of the study, and answered any questions about the project. At this time, the participants were asked if they were willing to be interviewed. When they agreed, the researcher asked the individuals to sign a consent form and to keep a copy of that form for their records.

At this stage of the first meeting, the researcher and the interviewee reached a mutual agreement about the time and the place of the interview. However, the researcher was not able to conduct that first meeting with each participant. For some participants, the first meeting was done over the phone due to the location and the time of the participants. Nevertheless, everything was the same, such as the rest of the participants' first meetings, except the part regarding the consent form. Phone interviewees signed their consent forms at the beginning of the actual research interviews. Each participant in this study was interviewed, face-to-face, for about an hour to answer the research questions. At least a three-day interval was utilized between the interviews. This period of time allowed the researcher to reflect on the interviews and to utilize new information for the following ones.

The interview session was held in a place and at a time mutually agreeable to the interviewer and the interviewee, and, accordingly, most of the interviews were held in the offices of the participants in their religious institutions and some were in their houses. Before conducting the actual interview, the researcher gave the interviewee the opportunity to ask any question about the study that might have come to mind since the first meeting. To make sure that the participant still knew the topic under investigation and the nature of the study, the researcher briefly repeated what was said in the first meeting, or over the phone, about the study and topics under investigation.

Each interview session started with a "grand tour question" about the nature of the participant's work as a religious leader in a sacred place. This kind of question and other general questions were needed to establish rapport with the interviewee. B. Berg (1995) considers such introductory questions as "ice breakers" prior to starting the real interview. Glesen and Peshkin (1993, p. 79) describe rapport as "tantamount to trust, and trust is the foundation for acquiring the fullest, most accurate disclosure a respondent is able to make."

Trust was a very crucial factor in this study. It encouraged participants to talk openly about the sensitive topic under investigation, terrorism. Thus, breaking the ice at the beginning of the interview session was crucial, not only because it allowed for smooth information flow, but also because it enhanced the validity of these data. After asking the general questions about interesting issues not related to the research topic and increasing the level of rapport, the actual interview questions were introduced.

The researcher followed careful procedures in collecting data to assure accurate and full accounts from the interviewees. These procedures included: first, objective and non-judgmental approach was used with the aim to understand, in as much detail as possible, the relevant aspects of the relationship between religion and terrorism; second, the researcher was always ready with a portable tape recorder, with extra tapes and batteries, and he had interviews audio-recorded with the participants' agreement; third, the interviewer avoided the sometimes intimidating atmosphere of formal interviews, and instead tried to carry out the interview as an informal conversation. At the end of the interview session, the researcher thanked the participant for his time and his contributions to the study.

DATA ANALYSIS

Careful attention was paid to how the raw interview data was analyzed in order to generate clear and logical findings. This research relied upon subjective information derived from in-depth and probing interviews. The analysis plan followed the sequence of the three ensuing strategies.

Verbatim Information Domains

First, at the initial data collection stage, the personal accounts and perceptions of spiritual leaders were organized into a minimum of eight strata comprising three Jewish groups (Orthodox, Conservative, and Reform); three Christian groups (Eastern Orthodox, Catholic, and Protestant); and two Muslim groups (Sunni and Shia). A minimum of three respondents was represented in each of the six strata in Judaism and Christianity. Four and two respondents were represented in the Sunni and Shia sects of Islam respectively. At this level of analysis, the transcribed information represented narrative data in its most basic state. This narrative reflected highly descriptive and full accounts of interviewee perceptions. Here, direct quotes provided verbatim and unmodified accounts of how the expert informants responded to the research questions. Although this stage illustrated the lowest level of data analysis, some direct quotes of subjects yet provided in-depth and significant explanation of the research questions in the nature of what C. Geertz (1973) calls "thick" description.

Collapsing to Case-Studies

A second level of analysis was met by identifying, within the verbatim narratives, selected cases or isolated and specific scenarios, which provided a higher level of organization of the transcriptions. It was impossible to predict precisely the number of relevant case studies which would illustrate different and novel responses to the research questions. However, cases emerged from the data to highlight how various religious leaders perceive and describe terrorism. A total of eight such specific case studies allowed for inclusion of all information domains, but such was unknown at the pre-data collection stage. Five to six reflected clearly divergent responses to terrorism, or various ways terrorism may be rationalized or condemned by one or more of the eight sub-strata of the religious groups. Regardless, with the case-studies' isolation, the researcher systematically made cross-case comparisons.

Emergence and Clarification of Themes

Both of the first two strategies (verbatim narratives and case studies) provided for "contextualizing" specific themes pertinent to religion and terrorism, which are deemed important in the review of literature and theoretical orientation. That is, how can a particular concept or theme (or research question) be explained by the respondents in the light of the larger cultural context which frames their worldview perception? In addition, how do the deep descriptive accounts of the participants give new meanings to pre-established concepts and ideas about religion and terrorism? Thus, for example, the concept of "rationalization" (of terrorism) may mean one thing to a rabbi and another to a Muslim sheikh. Such a phenomenon can only be understood in the context of the rabbi's or the sheikh's cultural backdrop gained in the subjectively-oriented interviews. At this stage of analysis, emphasis was on the isolation of themes most having been predicted by the review of literature; and some newly emerged from the primary data. A typology of pertinent themes was constructed to further clarify the overall relationship between religion and terrorism.

For this purpose, conceptual tables were constructed at this level illustrating the relationship between the variables (i.e., contrasting the eight religious sub-groups according to how terrorism may be rationalized or condemned).

Data analysis is an important part of the research process. Following qualitative strategies, data was collected, coded, organized, and analyzed on an ongoing basis. The primary method used in analyzing the data was content analysis. The researcher and two other doctoral students transcribed verbatim the interviews and created a manuscript for each participant.

After transcribing the interviews, the next step was to organize all the data accumulated in the interviews that were already conducted. This is, of course, the most exhausting and time-consuming process, even though it is also the most creative (Berg, 1995). Because qualitative research does not pertain to numbers that can be easily manipulated, qualitative analysis, therefore, "does not lend itself to this sort of certainty" (Berg, 1995, p. 59). The analysis plan of this study was based on Berg's (1995) recommendation and followed certain hints and tips on how to organize interview data. Thus the following steps were followed:

1. The data was arranged by establishing a filing system; each interview was filed separately. The file's cover had an information label that included the interviewee's name, date, time, and the subject matter. The tape-recorded material, as well as the transcription, consituted the file. This process gave easy access to data and various aspects of the data. Moreover, an identifiction number was given to each interviewee's file and transcripts. No one, other than the researcher, knew which identification number belonged to which participant.

2. After categorizing the data and classifying them into subcategories and subject matters according to the research questions, the data was analyzed to extract themes. Coding the data was the next step in the process of data analysis. This process led to a search for patterns, themes, and sub-categories of the data.

3. The data were arranged according to the types of research questions that were addressed to the subjects.

Furthermore, the answers were classified to each question as one discrete category. Finally, the results were deduced; the data were evaluated; a detailed description for each relevant item to religious-based terrorism was written; any relationship to theory was demonstrated. Accordingly, the findings of this study were presented and discussed; conclusions and recommendations were then presented.

VALIDITY AND RELIABILITY

Validity and reliability are important factors in any study. Usually we try to work on validity first, and then we should assure reliability. The researcher understands the traditional debate over these concepts between qualitative and quantitative research approaches. Many factors may affect validity and reliability, one of which is asking the right questions about the topic under investigation. To increase validity, however, the researcher used different questions aimed at gaining the same response. Questions were paraphrased in different ways to be directly related to terrorism and religious-based terrorism in order to maintain face validity. To increase content validity, questions were asked about perceptions toward different indicators of religious terrorism, such as bombing buildings, assassinations, suicide bombers, and hijacking. By increasing face and content validity, construct validity may also be increased.

Reliability is a constant concern. It means that one can expect the same results by using the same questions or the same instrument with similar subjects. In the qualitative paradigm, nevertheless, the researcher is the instrument; therefore, the right questions must be asked in different ways about the same topic to get identical responses using different approaches in order to increase reliability. The researcher, in this study, asked many questions about the same topic (religious-based terrorism) in different ways, and the questions were pre tested in pilot interviews as mentioned above.

Keeping in mind the problems of qualitative research, the researcher used an interview guide to ask the proper questions about the topic. Professors and peers reviewed the questions to check for any ambiguity in wording. The researcher pre-tested the questions with individuals from the three religions other than the participants to make sure that the questions were very clear; that is, in a pilot study. Finally, in the actual interview the researcher asked the interviewees if they needed more clarifications of the meaning of the questions. The researcher did not have any problem with these questions. The researcher, in many cases, paraphrased the participants' answers to make sure that they belonged to the right question. In so doing, the researcher minimized the effect of one of the major problems in qualitative research (i.e., not asking the right questions), which as a result can increase the validity and reliability of the study.

With regard to the problem that the participants might not share the information with the interviewer, the researcher tried to build a good rapport and trust with the participants. Once this goal is achieved, the participants are more willing to share information with the interviewer, which also has its positive reflections on the validity and reliability. The researcher, as a result of this method, maintained a good rapport with the participants. Many of them asked the researcher to keep in touch with them, and provided their personal cards with their home phone numbers. In some cases the researcher even was asked to be a guest lecturer in their religious institutions. In many cases also, some participants helped the researcher find other participants to take part in the study. Some of them even made all the phone calls and gave the researcher names of people who had already agreed to participate based on their recommendations. Thus, the researcher can claim that he maintained a good rapport with all the participants.

Honesty of the participants is another problem affecting reliability and validity in all "question-and-answer" studies. Although there is no single solution to the problem of honesty, maintaining trust, rapport, anonymity, and confidentiality can minimize the effect of this problem. As mentioned above, the researcher did his best to control these problems. In addition, the respondents' status in society, and their knowledge, increased the validity of this study. They are well-respected and influential people in their communities who often serve as decision makers and mediators.

A researcher's personal bias is another problem for validity, due to the role of the "researcher as an instrument." This researcher controlled this bias by using the following steps:

> 1. The interviewer strove to follow a nonjudgmental approach through all the stages of this study: designing and asking non-leading questions, collecting data objectively, transcribing, analyzing, and reporting the data.
> 2. The researcher remained neutral and did not give any negative or positive, verbal or nonverbal, feedback to what was reported by interviewees (for example, the researcher did not share his personal views about terrorism with the participants).
> 3. Finally, the researcher took the learner's role in conducting the interviews. He was a curious student who wanted to know and understand the religious leaders' perceptions on terrorism. The researcher did not introduce any prior knowledge about the topic to the interview session, and he took every piece of information said by participants as new knowledge about the topic. In other words, the researcher was a passive learner in each interview session.

LIMITATIONS

"The only perfect research is no research" (Hagan, 1993, p. 251). Hence, each study has its problems and limitations; this study is no exception. To explain, there are some limitations, due to the method itself, (i.e., the limitations of interviewing technique and the qualitative approach in general).

Also, the results of this study will not be generalizable to all religious leaders in the United States due to the sampling issues (non-probability sampling). However, the findings may be valid for those religious leaders who share the same characteristics and are in the same setting as the participants.

Moreover, this study is limited to self-report data (i.e., how participants perceive terrorism), which may have a potential self-report bias. Nevertheless, since participants reported or referred to certain religious books, as one of the questions required, another source of data became evident. This new source, religious publications, could be used to enhance the reliability and the validity of the study, and could be used as a kind of triangulation with the interview method. In other words, the data of this study are not limited only to personal perceptions of the participants; they also include perceptions and attitudes based on religious information from the holy books of these religions because the participants are experts in their religions.

The nature of the topic itself may be suggestive of limitations. Terrorism is a complicated and sensitive topic and one not easily defined. Consequently, the study is limited to how participants perceive and define terrorism. It is very difficult to find operational definitions of some variables pertinent to terrorism for possible quantification. Thus, a qualitative study, even with limitations, is more useful as a starting point.

This research, moreover, should provide conceptual clarity and allow for further hypothesizing and questionnaire design. Furthermore, the findings of this study may have three general implications. First, the study may contribute to the scarce scientific literature currently available about terrorism in general, and about religious-based terrorism in particular.

Second, this study may help some people to affirm or refute the stereotypes about the role of religious leaders in the area of terrorism, and the use of religion as a motive in terrorism. The media are focusing on the role of some religious leaders in many terrorist incidents around the world and more knowledge about the traditional, less extreme beliefs may help demythologize public perceptions of these religions.

Third, the study could assist policymakers in formulating plans to deal with this kind of criminal violence, not only in the United States but also in other countries that face the problem of terrorism motivated by religion. Whether or not religious leaders play a positive or negative role in promoting terrorism, findings of this study will help policymakers and law enforcement agencies in understanding religious-based terrorism.

HUMAN SUBJECTS' PROTECTION

Participants in this study, as well as in any study, are the most important factor because without them there is no study. Therefore, the researcher did his best to protect his participants against any potential risk. Voluntary participation, no harm to the participants, anonymity, and confidentiality are the most common ethical considerations in social research (Babbie, 1995).

The ethical considerations were understood and the following procedures were taken to assure the participants' protection and to maintain the ethical issues:

> 1. The Indiana University of Pennsylvania (IUP) Institutional Review Board (IRB) approved this study. This approval was mentioned to the participants as evidence of the ethical considerations toward them from both the researcher

and IUP.

2. Voluntary participation in this study was maintained by allowing the participants to withdraw at any time simply by ending the interview session. Luckily, all participants completed their interviews and no one withdrew from the study. Moreover, informed consent forms were given to the participants to sign before conducting the interview. The consent form contained the following elements:

(a) Participation in the study is VOLUNTARY.

(b) The subject may withdraw from the interview at any time, simply by so advising the researcher. This withdrawal will not cause any negative consequences to the subject.

(c) There is NO KNOWN risk as a result of the participation in the study.

(d) The confidentiality of the information is maintained.

(e) The researcher requests that the interview be audiotaped.

3. When the participant agreed to take part in the project, a time and a place convenient to the researcher and the interviewee were arranged to conduct the actual interview. There was no harm or risk to the participants. There was no known risk that would result from participation in this study. However, the participants might have been reluctant to make any statements which could be misinterpreted and which could lead to questioning by law enforcement officials. The researcher minimized this risk by establishing a good rapport and trust with the participants. Minimizing this risk not only protected the participants but also will increase the validity and reliability of the study.

Although there was no known risk as a result of participation in this study, the nature of the method (interview) did not specify every question to be asked in advance, which created the potential for of asking risky questions on the spot. To avoid this risk, the researcher did not ask sensitive or personal questions seeking direct involvement in terrorism. The researcher has a professional background (seventeen years of employment in federal law enforcement in Jordan) that helped him avoid asking sensitive questions about the topic under research.

In addition, all participants were in a position to decide how much personal information they wanted to disclose. Given their roles in society as religious leaders, they were qualified to reduce any potential risk from taking part in this study or answering specific questions. Finally, participants were given the choice not to answer any question they would find too sensitive or involving risky results.

4. Confidentiality. The researcher is aware of the requirement of protection of human subjects and the ethics and responsibilities of research. Graduate coursework in the Department of Criminology provided a close awareness of ethical considerations of research and the critical role of the IRB in protecting the participants. The following steps were taken to protect the subjects and to maintain confidentiality:

(a) The researcher, personally, conducted the interviews, and he transcribed most of the interviews of this study. Although the researcher did give some interviews to two other individuals for transcription, he did not provide them with any personal identifiers of those interviewees. The researcher gave just the tapes without any names or locations of those who were taped. The two persons who did the transcription were also doctoral students and aware of the requirements of human subjects protection. Yet, the researcher asked them not to reveal any information about the tapes, and they promised to do that.

(b) Each participant was assigned an ID number and given a file containing the transcription of the interview. No one other than the researcher knew which number identifies which subject.

(c) The researcher did not release any information concerning the subjects' identifiers. During transcribing the interviews, all identifying information, such as names of participants, places of work, or any other personal information, were deleted. In other words, this kind of information did not appear in the transcriptions of the interviews.

(d) The researcher did not attribute quotes or comments to any participant by name or address of work.

References

Aho, J. (1990). *The Politics of Righteousness: Idaho Christian Patriotism.* Seattle: University of Washington.

Albanese, J. (1993). *Crime in America.* Englewood Cliffs, NJ: Regents/Prentice.

Austin, T. (1989). Living on the edge: The impact of terrorism upon Philippine villagers. *International Journal of Offender Therapy and Comparative Criminology,* 33 (1), 103–119.

Austin, T. (1991). Toward a theory on the impact of terrorism. *International Journal of Comparative and Applied Criminal Justice,* 15 (1), 33–48.

Austin, T. (1996). Banana justice in Moroland: Peace making in mixed Muslim Christian towns in Southern Philippines. In C. Field & R. Moore (Eds.), *Comparative Criminal Justice: Traditional and Nontraditional Systems of Law and Control* (pp. 270–291). Prospect Heights, IL: Waveland.

Austin, T. (1999). *Banana Justice: Field Notes on Philippine Crime and Custom.* Westport, CT: Praeger.

Babbie, E. (1990). *Survey Research Methods* (2nd ed.). Belmont, CA: Wadsworth.

Babbie, E. (1995). *The Practice of Social Research* (7th ed.). Belmont, CA: Wadsworth.

Barghothi, J. (1996). International terrorism in historical perspective. In C. Fields & R. Moore (Eds.), *Comparative Criminal Justice: Traditional and Nontraditional Systems of Law and Control* (pp.83–96). Prospect Heights, IL: Waveland.

Berg, B. (1995). *Qualitative Research Methods for Social Science* (2nd ed.). Boston: Allyn & Bacon.

Bodansky, Y. (1993). *Target America: Terrorism in the U.S. Today.* New York: S.P.I Books.

Cetron, M. (1989). The growing threat of terrorism. *The Futurist,* 23, 20–24.

Corbett, J. (1994). *Religion in America* (2nd ed). Englewood Cliffs, NJ: Prentice–Hall.

Currn, D., & Rezetti, C. (1994). *Theories of Crime.* Needham, MA: Allyn & Bacon.

Daher, A. (1994). *Alirhab Alalmei: Irhab Aldowal, Dowal wa Amlyat Alirhab* (Global terrorism: States' terrorism, states and operations of terrorism). Beirut, Lebanon: Dar Alhosam.

Durkheim, E. (1951). *Suicide: A Study in Sociology* (J. Spaulding & G. Simpson, Trans.). New York: Free Press. (Original work published in 1897.)

Eagan, S. (1996). From spikes to bombs: The rise of Eco–Terrorism. *Studies in Conflict and Terrorism*, 19, 1–18.

Eitzen, D & Zinn, W. (1988). *In Conflict and Order*. Newtown, MA: Allyn & Bacon.

Esposito, J. (1995). *The Islamic Threat: Myth or Reality* (2nd ed.). New York: Oxford University Press.

Ezeldin, A. (1990). *Global Terrorism: An Overview*. Chicago: University of Illinois.

Friedlander, R. (1979). *Terrorism*. New York: Ocean Publishers.

Gallagher, E. (1997). God and country: Revolution as religious imperative on the radical right. *Terrorism and Political Violence*, 9 (3), 63–79.

Geertz, C. (1973). *The Interpretation of Cultures*. New York: Basic Books.

George, J. & Wilcox, L. (1992). *Nazis, Communists, Klansmen and Others on the Fringe: Political extremism in America*. Buffalo, NY: Prometheus Books.

Gibbs, J. (1989). Conceptualization of terrorism. *American Sociological Review*, 54, 329–340.

Glesne, C., & Peshkin, A. (1993). *Becoming Qualitative Researchers: An Introduction*. New York: Longman.

Gurr, T. (1988). Political terrorism in the United States: Historical and contemporary trends. In M. Stohl (Ed.), *The Politics of Terrorism*. New York: Marcel Dekker.

Hagan, F. (1993). *Research Methods in Criminal Justice and Criminology* (3rd ed.). New York: Macmillan.

Hanauer, L. (1995). The path to redemption: Fundamentalist Judaism, territory, and Jewish settler violence in the West Bank. *Studies in Conflict and Terrorism*, 18, 245–270.

Harris, J. (1987). Domestic terrorism in the 1980s. *FBI Law Enforcement Bulletin*, 56 (11), 5–13.

Hoffman, B. (1988). *Recent Trends and Future Prospects of Terrorism*. Santa Monica, CA: Rand.

Hoffman, B. (1995). "Holy Terror": The implications of terrorism motivated by a religious imperative. *Studies in Conflict and Terrorism*, 18, 271–284.

Hoffman, B. (1997). The confluence of international and domestic terrorism. *Terrorism and Political Violence*, 9 (2), 1–15.

Holden, R. (1987). Conservatism, fundamentalism and identity theology: The road to religious extremism. *Paper Presented at the Academy of Criminal Justice Sciences*, St. Louis, MO (March).

Hyman, A. (1994). Muslim fundamentalism. In Y. Alexander (Ed.), *Middle East Terrorism: Current Threats and Future Prospects* (pp. 233–260). New York: G.K. Hall.

Israeli, R. (1997). Islamikaze and their significance. *Terrorism and Political Violence*, 9 (3), 96–121.

Juergensmeyer, M. (1997). Terror mandated by God. *Terrorism and Political Violence*, 9 (2), 16–23.

Kaplan, J. (1997). Leaderless resistance. *Terrorism and Political Violence*, 9 (3), 80–95.

Karabell, Z. (1995). The wrong threat. *World Policy Journal*, 12 (2), 37–48.

Kellen, K. (1982). *On Terrorists and Terrorism*. Santa Monica, CA: Rand.

Kelly, J., & Cook, W. (1995). Extremism and fundamentalism: The return to paradise. *Journal of Contemporary Criminal Justice*, 11, 14–34.

Kidder, R. (1993). The terrorist mentality. In B. Schechterman & M. Slann (Eds.), *Violence and Terrorism* (3rd ed.), pp. 30–32. Guilford, CT: Dushkin.

Kissmane, T. (1989). *The Theoretical Literature on Terrorism: A Sociological Interpretation*. Unpublished doctoral dissertation, Fordham University, New York.

Kupperman, R. (1986). Terrorism and traditional security. *Terrorism: An International Journal*, 8, 255–261.

Laqueur, W. (1977). *Terrorism*. Boston: Little, Brown.

Laqueur, W. (1987). *The Age of Terrorism*. Boston: Little, Brown and Company.

Laqueur, W. (1996). Post modern terrorism. *Foreign Affairs*, 75 (5), 24–36.

Lewis, B. (1967). *The Assassins: A Radical Sect in Islam*. London: Weidenfeld and Nicolson.

Looke, L., Spirdudo, W., & Silverman, S. (1993). *Proposals that Work: A Guide for Planning Dissertations and Grant Proposals*. Newbury Park, CA: Sage.

Marshall, C., & Rossman, C. (1989). *Designing Qualitative Research*. Newbury Park, CA: Sage.

Martin, J. (1988). The study of crime: A criminal justice perspective. *Criminal Justice International*, 4 (2), 1–8.

Martin, R., Mutchnick, R., & Austin, W. (1990). *Criminological Thought: Pioneers Past and Present*. New York: Macmillan.

Mazrui, A. (1996). Between the crescent and the star-spangled banner: American Muslims and U.S. foreign policy. *International Affairs*, 73, 491–506.

Merton, R. (1957). Social structure and anomie. In R. Merton (Ed.), *Social Theory and Social Structure* (rev. ed., pp.131–160). New York: Free Press of Glencoe.

Merton, R. (1997). On the evolving synthesis of differential association and anomie theory: A perspective from the sociology of science. *Criminology*, 35 (3), 517–525.

Mullins, W. (1988). Stopping terrorism. *Journal of Contemporary Criminal Justice*, 4 (4), 214–228.

Mullins, W. (1997). *A Sourcebook on Domestic and International Terrorism: An Analysis of Issues, Organizations, Tactics, and Responses* (2nd ed). Springfield, IL: Charles C. Thomas.

Mutchnick, R. & Berg, B. (1996). *Research Methods for the Social Sciences: Practice and Applications*. Needham Heights, MA: Allyn & Bacon.

Parrinder, G. (1971). *World Religions: From Ancient History to Present*. New York: Facts On File.

Perry, S. (1997). The un–civil war. *Crime and Justice International*, 13 (1), 3–17.

Public Law 104–132. *Antiterrorism and Effective Death Penalty Act of 1996*. United States: 104th Congress.

Ranstorp, M. (1996). Terrorism in the name of religion. *Journal of International Affairs*, 50 (1), 41–62.

Rapoport, D. (1984). Fear and trembling: Terrorism in three religious traditions. *American Political Science Review*, 78, 658–677.

Rapoport, D. (1988). Messianic sanctions for terror. *Comparative Politics*, 20, 195–213.

Revell, O. (1987). Terrorism today. *FBI Law Enforcement Bulletin*, 56 (11), 1–4.

Rubin, H., & Rubin, I. (1995). *Qualitative Interviewing: The Art of Hearing Data*. Thousand Oaks, CA: Sage.

Sabig, S. (1984). *Figeh al–Sunnah* (Theology of Sunni). Ryyad, Saudi Arabia: Maktabat alkhadmat alhadiethah.

Sandler, T. (1993). The effectiveness of antiterrorism policies. *American Political Science Review*, 4, 829–844.

Schbley, A. (1990). Religious terrorists: What they aren't going to tell us. *Terrorism*, 13, 3, 237–241.

Schechterman, B., & Slann, M. (1998). *Violence and Terrorism* (4th ed.). Guilford, CT: Dushkin/McGraw–Hill.

Schmid, A. (1983). *Political Terrorism: A Research Guide to Concept, Theories, Data Bases, and Literature*. Amsterdam: North Holland Publishers.

Sederberg, P. (1991). Responses to terrorism. In Schechterman, B., & Slann, M. (Eds.), *Violence and Terrorism* (pp. 6–9). Guilford, CT: Dushkin.

Seidman, I. (1991). *Interviewing as Qualitative Research*. New York: Teachers College Press.

Shukry, M. (1991). *Al–irhab Al–dowly* (International Terrorism). Beirut, Lebanon: Dar Alilm Lilmalayein.

Shultz, R., & Schmauder, J. (1994). Emerging regional conflicts and U.S. in the 1990s. *Studies in Conflict and Terrorism*, 17, 1–22.

Smith, J. & Morgan, K. (1994). Terrorist right and left: Empirical issues in profiling American terrorists. *Studies in Conflict and Terrorism*, 54 (9), 62–66.

Stinson, J. (1987). Domestic terrorism in the United States. *The Police Chief*, 54 (9), 62–66.

Sykes, G., & Matza, D. (1957). Techniques of neutralization: A theory of delinquency. *American Sociological Review*, 22, 664–670.

U.S. Department of Justice. (1993). Terrorism in the United States. FBI: Terrorist Research Center.

U.S. Department of State. (2001). *Patterns of Global Terrorism 2000*. Office of the Coordinator for Counterterrorism, April 2001.

Vyver, J. (1996). Religious fundamentalism and human rights. *Journal of International Affairs*, 50 (1), 21–40.

White, J. (1986). *Holy War: Terrorism as a Theological Construct*. Gaithersburg, MD: IACP.

White, J. (1991). *Terrorism: an Introduction*. Belmont, CA: Wadsworth.

Yerushalmi, M. (1987). A control code model of terrorism. In Ward & Smith (Eds.), *International Terrorism: The Domestic Response* (pp. 77–83). Chicago: University of Illinois.

Index

About the Author

AREF M. AL-KHATTAR is an Associate Professor of Criminology and Criminal Justice at California University of Pennsylvania.